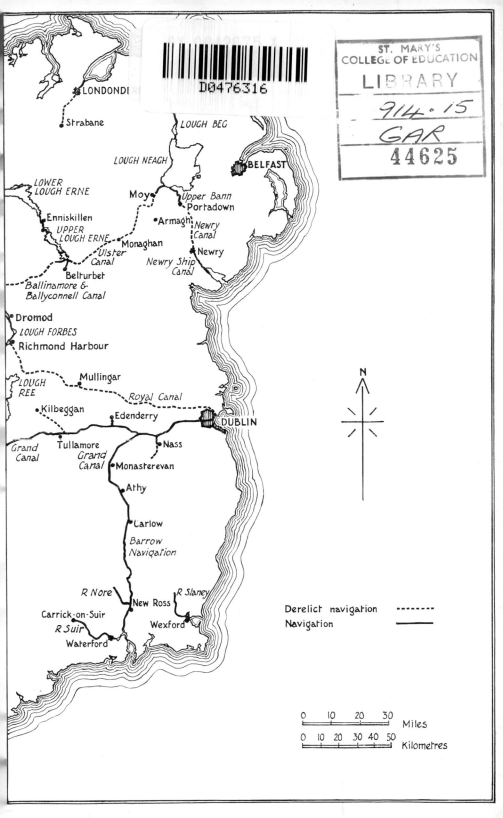

ST. MARY'S
COLLEGE OF EDUCATION
LIBRARY
914·15
GAR
44625

LONDONDE

Strabane

LOUGH BEG

LOUGH NEAGH

BELFAST

LOWER
LOUGH ERNE

Moy

Upper Bann
Portadown

Enniskillen

Armagh

Newry
Canal

UPPER
LOUGH ERNE

Monaghan

Ulster
Canal

Newry

Newry Ship
Canal

Belturbet

Ballinamore &
Ballyconnell Canal

Dromod

LOUGH FORBES

Richmond Harbour

Mullingar

LOUGH
REE

Royal Canal

Kilbeggan

Edenderry

DUBLIN

Tullamore

Nass

Grand
Canal

Grand
Canal

Monasterevan

Athy

Carlow

Barrow
Navigation

R Nore

R Slaney

New Ross

Carrick-on-Suir

Wexford

R Suir

Waterford

N

Derelict navigation ----------
Navigation _____

0   10   20   30
Miles
0 10 20 30 40 50
Kilometres

Land of Time Enough

ST. MARY'S COLLEGE OF EDUCATION
LIBRARY

Date Due	Date Due	Date Due

Land of Time Enough

by

Raymond Gardner

HODDER AND STOUGHTON

LONDON   SYDNEY   AUCKLAND   TORONTO

44625

Copyright © 1977 by Raymond Gardner. First printed 1977. ISBN 0 340 21745 6.
All rights reserved. No part of this publication may be reproduced or transmitted in
any form or by any means, electronic or mechanical, including photocopy, recording,
or any information storage and retrieval system, without permission in writing from
the publisher. Printed in Great Britain for Hodder and Stoughton Limited, Mill
Road, Dunton Green, Sevenoaks, Kent, by Ebenezer Baylis and Son Limited, The
Trinity Press, Worcester, and London. Hodder and Stoughton Editorial Office: 47
Bedford Square, London WC1B 3DP

To MALCOLM who planted the idea

To ERIC who nurtured it

Above all, to VAL who put up with it

Acknowledgments

THIS BOOK COULD NOT have been written without the assistance of the following organisations: Emerald Star Line, owners of *Fenniscourt Star*; Bord na Mona; Bord Fáilte Eireann; Bord Solathair An Leictreachais; Córas Iompair Eireann; B and I Line; the National Library of Ireland. I should like to thank all those members of the Inland Waterways Association of Ireland without whose vigorous campaign to retain the navigations our voyage would have run aground.

Many individuals gave freely of their time in the research: Ted Barrett, Gay and Frank Blake, Very Rev. C. B. Champ, Dean of Clonfert, Bill Duggan, N. W. English, A. Eyre Chatterton, Tommy Gladney, L. M. Goodbody, Ruth Heard, Vivien Igoe, Dom Kearns, the Lefroy family, Tom Maher, Cecil Miller, Harman Murtagh, Kathryn Neilson, Rusty and George Speirs, Heather and Mike Thomas, John Weaving (Twiggy and Brocky), Eugene Spollen, Mrs. Marjorie Waller, and Joe Wynne.

Finally I should like to thank those who enriched our voyage and its design with their wit, unstinted encouragement and abundant hospitality: Deirdre and Jeremy Addis, Peggy and Brendan Daly, Ida and Derek Dann, Ann and John McNamara and Trevor West. They were all on the side of the angels.

Author's note

The anglicising of Irish place names has caused a great deal of chaos on maps of Ireland on which many variants are to be found. I have attempted to use the most common spelling and where the original Irish may be significant I have given it and the interpretation used by P. W. Joyce in *The History and Origin of Irish Names of Places* (E. P. Publishing)

Contents

Illustrations

ILLUSTRATIONS

Acknowledgements
1 W. M. Nixon
2 Desmond Simmons, executor of John O. Simmons' estate
3 Bord Fáilte Eireann
4 Jeremy Addis
5 Córas Iompair Eireann
6 Arthur Guinness, Son & Co., Ltd.
7 John Conway

Part I

In August of each year, for a considerable time past, a regatta has been held upon Lough Ree. Hither flock the fashion and beauty of the district for miles around; and once more a fleet enlivens the aspect of the usually deserted lake. Gay vessels decorated with many-coloured streamers, accompanied by bands of music, and laden with gentlest ladies and gallant gentlemen glide tranquilly over the scene of many a well-contested battle.

—from *Three Days on the Shannon* by W. F. Wakeman, published in 1852

ONE

River of Destiny

THIS IS THE STORY of a love affair with a river discovered after many years of adventure on the waterways of England. The proportions of the Shannon, the variety of its scenery, the breadth of its history and legend, and the warmth of the welcome with which Val and I were met make Shannonside a hard land to equal. We were to find a parallel on the River Barrow, also in Ireland, but that was yet to come.

On our visits across the Irish Sea we took that road which leads from Dublin to Galway in the west along the ridge of gravel hills, the Esker Riada, which has afforded the traveller safe passage across the bog-strewn central bowl of Ireland since pre-Christian times. Although we respected local custom and drove at snail's pace through the streets of Athlone, we never dallied in our haste to greet the Atlantic, the mountains of Connemara, our beloved Aran Islands with their tales of the Fir Bolg, Atlantis and great dry stone dykes and fortifications of such antiquity that no man has ever proven their age or use. And when September came we would travel south round Galway Bay and take the road which leads to the oyster beds and Moran's Bar. There we would consume great quantities of stout and even greater quantities of the first free-bed oysters of the season.

One year we were in Ireland in the middle of an "R-less" series of months. Without the prospect of an oyster in sight we headed north to Westport, an unexpectedly Georgian town, built to a plan by James Wyatt, and left almost undisturbed since to make it the most elegant small town in the country. From there we travelled east along a different road to Dublin. It led us through Carrick on Shannon and here we discovered the river which more than one hundred miles later would be immortalised as, "the spacious Shenan spreading like a sea," as Spenser had it in *The Faerie Queen*. The weather was glorious and we sat on the bank beside the bridge to watch the sculls pass and the pleasure craft moor to the jetty.

In England the people of the canals had a name for those who lazed and watched the efforts of others; they called them gongoozlers. We were unashamed gongoozlers that day. It was the day when our dog gave way to the primeval instinct to obliterate her scent by rolling in a much decomposed Shannon fish. She took not at all to being slung into the water and scrubbed down with a broom borrowed from one of the moored craft. Undaunted, we vowed to return and search out the secrets of this enchanted waterway.

The following year we were back and took to the water for one week. We remained for three. Today the Shannon is our obsession. No matter how many times we make the passage from Carrick south to Killaloe, or north into the Boyle river and Lough Key, there is always some new village, creek, island, story-teller or musician to be found. And there are few occasions when we are not offered some special discovery, whether it be a new song or story, or perhaps just another version of a story we were told the previous year. Perhaps we will come across another crumbling harbour. (Who used it? When did the last steamer call?); or the ruined home of an island monk in the middle of a lough (Who was he? When did he live?); or just another bare Irish bar with people for furniture. It was in such a place, at Garrykennedy, that we were entertained to the music of Gerry Martin and a great massed band of fiddlers aged from nine to ninety. In the middle sat Mr. Martin, past ninety, making fiddles all day in his village home and playing them all night until the Garda called time.

Let us not hasten into the stream too soon. For just as surely as the course of the Shannon follows the course of Irish history, we were soon to discover that the great wealth of this river would not be given up to some speedboat tripper determined to say that he had "done the Shannon", by which he meant that he had cruised its length in the shortest possible time with one eye on the fuel gauge, another on the compass and a cursory glance at the odd ruin through binoculars. Time and again we met the waterhogs at the village inn of an evening. One such character convinced us that there was no room for people on his craft, that it was simply a floating fuel tank and engine. He might as well have been on Mars. They have canals there too.

Then let us give the Shannon its due and go where no boat may venture; to the wild and stormy heights on the borderlands of Cavan and Fermanagh where we find the pool they call Lugnashina or The Shannon Pot. In Irish it is Lug na Sionna, the Hollow or Hole of the Shannon. This is the source of our adventure. And as the Shannon departs we find that this stream, dropping sharply through 340 feet in a distance of only nine miles to the head of Lough Allen, is the prelude to the longest river in these islands. This is no ordinary river but a series of narrow sections and canalised pounds linking a number of lakes. Some are small and tranquil, others tempestuous in even the slightest breeze. Lough Derg runs for more than twenty-four miles from Portumna in County Galway to Killaloe in Clare where man has tamed the waters to tumble and boil through the head race and serve the turbines at Ardnacrusha hydro-electric station just upstream from Limerick. It is an unsightly end. There is enough before.

First there is the name. Worthy but dour historians such as William Camden have suggested that the name derives from Sean Abhainn, Old River. But there are finer accounts in the annals of the past. There was once a poet who ruled Ireland and some of his work has been preserved in the *Book of Leinster*. He has a story of the origin of the Shannon's name.

Around a well, known as Connla's, grew nine hazel trees from the branches of which hung the mystical nuts which held the secret to all that was best in literature, poetry and art. When they fell into the pool the nuts were gobbled by the salmon to give them their red dappled belly-markings, and us the legend of the salmon of wisdom. Men who had prepared themselves with the appropriate rite partook of the salmon and thus of the knowledge that it would be a bad thing if any woman should become so well educated. They made Connla's well a *gessa*, a place taboo to women. But was not Sionnain the grand-daughter of the Gael's sea god Ler? What man might deny her right to the source of this knowledge? Sionnain went to the well. The salmon were so enraged that they whipped the pool to a cauldron which overflowed into nine streams. One stream devoured Sionnain and the waters rushed on to form the river we call the Shannon.

This was the time of the Land Beneath the Waves and some have suggested that Sionnain was swept into the Land of the Mortals. It is as fair an account of the naming of the Shannon as we have come across. Its most modern occurrence is not in Irish literature at all but in the work of the Scottish writer Neil Gunn, who died in 1973. Gunn, the son of a crofter-fisherman from Latheron in Caithness, spent much of his life collecting the folk tales of his land. These stories of remote but enduring communities, like many to be found in Ireland, were translated into his novels and fantasies. For Gunn the Land Beneath the Waves became *The Green Isle of the Great Deep*. Here is the place into which Hector and Art are swept after the boy climbs the hazel tree and Hector attempts to lure the salmon with a broken hazel bough.

Old Hector looked as if he might talk now to Art of many things and times of long ago. In the moment they could wait, all of life could be told. A strange and silent smile, such as Art had never before seen, glimmered on his face, and in that moment Art entered into his heritage and he loved Old Hector and the presence of all those who had been here before, alive or dead. The creases gathered on one side of Old Hector's face in a fabulous wink. Life is good, too! Then he smiled to Art, looking at him alone, and Art could not speak.

Instead he looked at the deep hole before him.

"How deep is it?" he asked softly.

"So deep," murmured Old Hector, "that we could only come out through the bottom."

"Where?"

"In the Green Isle of the Great Deep."

Irish tales of the salmon of wisdom abound. In the Fenian legends the heroic Finn, the fair one, attends a poet in order to learn his art. The poet had spent many years waiting for the salmon and when he caught it he gave it to Finn to cook. Although the boy had been warned to eat none of the flesh, it is told that he burned his hand and stuck his fingers in his mouth to cool them. From then on whenever Finn was in need of help, he would stick his fingers in his mouth and his problems would be resolved.

Such succulent knowledge is hard to come by these days, but, although I cannot vouch for the authenticity of these tales, I can recommend the qualities of the salmon's kin which now swim in the Shannon. Many is the brown paper parcel which has appeared from beneath the bar counter when our credentials have been put to the test over a few jars of stout. And many is the gourmet meal we have enjoyed after closing time.

Back in the twentieth century navigation of the Shannon begins at Battlebridge where the river, having passed out of Lough Allen, changes from a boulder-strewn torrent to a narrow, winding, but passable waterway. On one of our early Shannon voyages we were determined to visit Lough Allen. It was the summer of 1975, a strange time when Western Europe was bathed in sunshine and England prepared for 1976, the year of the potato at fifteen pence per pound. In Ireland the newspapers were marshalling their leader columns against the Government's decision not to import potatoes from Cyprus since their native crop was failing to meet demand. The Government withdrew import restrictions. I remember mooring to the old quay at Leitrim, just south of Battlebridge, and spending the entire evening in the bar describing the boiling capacities, taste and texture of the Cyprus potato.

Leitrim was the place where our hound, a diminutive bitch of the type best described as 57 varieties, exceeded her capacity for stout. Such was the astonishment of the drinkers at my description of a slimy rather than a floury food, that they had rested their glasses on the floor. These were drained by our dog who was discovered lurching about the quay. She fell in, was fished out, and spent the rest of the night recovering before the fire. I have since sworn never

ST. MARY'S COLLEGE OF EDUCATION
FALLS ROAD, BELFAST, 12.

to tell tales about potatoes in an Irish bar. One dog has been on the wagon ever since.

I digress. But digression is the basic spirit of Irish hospitality and if the stranger finds the habit brushing off on him he should rejoice and welcome it as a beneficial adjunct to his visit. They say it takes an American a week to slow down to the pace of life in Ireland. It takes a Britisher four days. But back to Lough Allen. On that hot June day, with the temperature in the eighties, the lake seemed a long way from Battlebridge, to which we had cruised in the dinghy. Here we found a great bustle of activity as men with drills bored into the original lock cill. They were preparing to open the long derelict Lough Allen canal as far as Acres Lough and had already cleaned and restored the basin above the first lock. As we walked along the narrow metalled road which runs beside the canal we heard the sound of trees being drawn up by their roots and came across an earth-mover working along the opposite bank, clearing more than forty years of reed and briar from the bed of the waterway.

At the next lock, Drumleague, we came upon another party of what must be the last band of professional navigators in Ireland. They were up to their knees in mud at the bottom of the empty lock but, as it lay partly beneath a bridge, they were at least sheltered from the blazing sun. As we left the road and tried to beat our way through the still uncleared briars of the line, as the towpath is known in Ireland, we knew defeat. We picnicked where we were and then made our way across a miniature bog to rejoin the road. A passing cyclist told us that we were still a good six miles from Lough Allen and whether these were English miles, or longer Irish miles, or still longer Irish miles of the imagination, did not matter at all. We began the slow walk back.

We met an elderly couple by a roadside pump. They were filling pails with water and told us that the piped water had failed due to the drought and that they had to walk more than half a mile from their homestead to fill the buckets. We blethered for an hour or so, not a bad average for casual Shannonside meetings. I remember that the old man would not let our dog drink from his pail, although his own hound was permitted to do so. He said he was not sure about foreign dogs, or where they had been. I agreed to this point although, considering the roistering of the previous evening, I should have thought that our own specimen was well disinfected.

Early the following morning, in search of an appetite to justify the huge breakfasts we liked to eat on board, we went for a stroll along the line of the derelict Ballinamore and Ballyconnell Canal which enters the Shannon at Leitrim. The canal used to provide a through route between the major waters of the Shannon and the Erne.

Inland navigation construction in Ireland was a haphazard affair. A number of waterways were designed as drainage schemes and converted to navigable channels at the last minute; others were built to provide famine relief rather than out of a need for a transport link. The failures stare at one from a waterway map of the country — in the form of dotted lines marked derelict. The Ballinamore and Ballyconnell was started in June 1846 and completed, to the point where through passage was possible with difficulty, in 1860 when the Commissioners of Public Works handed over control to a body of trustees. Local people talk of no more than half a dozen craft navigating its full length until 1870, after which time maintenance was abandoned. Even the canal's official historian, Richard Flanagan, has only been able to increase that figure to fifteen craft. By the 1870s, the railways were providing faster and more direct communication.

By 1906 one of the trustees was to write that it was "a farce calling it a navigation". Interest has been rekindled, since the extensive use of both the Shannon and the Erne as cruising waterways would make the reopening of the canal a useful enterprise. Leitrim County, with an eye on the tourist trade from the river, would welcome the appearance of craft striking across an area dependent on agriculture and tourism. The Inland Waterways Association of Ireland is also a champion of the reopening. There are those who suggest that the troubles between Ulster and the Republic are sufficient to staunch any further discussion of the project but as an Irish Press editorial pointed out as late as 1971: "If the Americans can cross the world to play ping-pong after Korea, the Irish have not alone an opportunity but a duty to show themselves mature enough to establish this bridge over troubled waters."

The Ballinamore and Ballyconnell's early history by no means makes it the most amazing white elephant of the system. That distinction is reserved for the canal at Cong, the unkindest cut of all as I like to call it. Loughs Mask and Corrib are connected by underground rivers, an indication of permeable ground which might give cause for thought to any water engineer. Nothing so obvious was considered by the Government when, to relieve famine in 1846, they decided to build a link between the lakes. Here is Sir William Wilde's archaic but succinct account of the procedure, written in 1867:

> A project was entertained of opening up a free communication through the great chain of lakes — Corrib, Mask and Carra — with the harbour of Galway (like the Caledonian Canal), and much expense was incurred in constructing a canal, locks and other works for that purpose. Before they were completed, it turned out to be a failure . . . for it was discovered that, like many other undertakings, the great canal at Cong "would not hold water". There it remains among the ruins of Cong, so dry that little boys may be seen playing marbles on the bottom.

The Shannon begins to assert a regal and devious nature as it winds slowly beneath the bridge at Carrick. Entering Lough Corry the waterborne traveller discovers, to his consternation or pleasure — depending on how well he has examined the charts beforehand — one of the stranger aspects of the small lakes. On our first cruise, just half an hour's journey from the town, we thought that some freak growth had closed the navigable channel south from the lake. In vain we searched for the channel and it was not until we caught a glimpse of the gleaming superstructure of another craft, seemingly ploughing through the reeds and then saw her bow cresting round the point, that we discovered the course. Such was the depth and height of the reed line that it appeared, even with powerful binoculars, to stretch across the channel until we were upon the cutting.

As the course of the Shannon demands respect from the helmsman so its legends will engage the mind of the most desultory traveller. The scholar might do worse than spend a period of his studies meandering its length. If he travelled by boat he would be moving in the wake of those whose past he seeks. At almost every town and village there is cause to question. How did Portumna (Port Omna) come to earn its name which means the Port of the Tree Trunk. How did Carrick, Carra Droma Ruisc, come to be translated as the Weir of the Marshy Ridge.

In one story of the place called Athlone, which lies on the river just south of Lough Ree, it is said that there was a man called Luan mac Luighdeach – Luan, the son of Levy – who kept an inn near the ford. In time the place came to be known as Ath Luan, the Town of the Ford of Luan. But there is another tale which accounts for the naming of this strategic town sitting astride the main thoroughfare across Ireland, a road which gave rise to the description of the place as "the key to Connacht". The legend begins before the written history of Ireland and was first recorded when chronological manuscripts were prepared by Celtic scholars in the eighth century. By this time the tale had become the work of many hands and minds. Our story comes from the Irish epic *Tain Bo Cuailnge*, the Cattle Raid of Cooley, a territory in the province of Ulster.

John Weaving, who plies to and fro on the river building jetties and maintaining harbours, and who was to play a great part in enchanting us with his river, told us the story as he educated us in a wealth of Irish myth and legend when we met him on our travels. We were in the inn at Garrykennedy and the tale became more complicated as many an imbiber added his own embellishments. In the end we found a copy of Thomas Kinsella's eloquent English translation of the manuscripts dating from the eighth and twelfth centuries. It is a book as gripping as any modern war history, and one which few readers will be able to put down once they have been caught by the story of the two great bulls.

It is Ireland before the fifth century. Maeve was Queen of Connacht and her marriage to Ailill was a lively one. Both were frequently at loggerheads over the question of who owned the greater wealth. The row reached a climax and both agreed to set out all they owned for measurement. Both were found to be equal with one exception. The King had a great white bull called Finnbennach Ai (the white one). Maeve, not to be outdone, commanded the messenger Mac Roth to scour the land for the white bull's equal. Mac Roth discovered Donn Cuailnge (the brown one) owned by Daire mac Fiachna and Maeve promised all manner of rewards to the Ulsterman if she might borrow his bull. Not surprisingly mac Fiachna agreed to the loan since Maeve not only offered many cattle and lands for his trouble but also her "own friendly thighs on top of that".

But some members of Mac Roth's band spoke out of turn while being entertained in Ulster and their host heard that had he not agreed to the loan, the bull would have been taken by force. Not even the promise of Maeve's graces and favours diminished the insult. And so the Provinces of Ireland went to war. In time the bulls Finnbennach Ai and Donn Cuailnge met on Ai Plain at Tarbga and a great bellowing and stamping beset the land and did not end until Donn Cuailnge picked up the dead body of his foe on his horns. At Cruachan he went into the water and emerged with Finnbennach Ai's loins, shoulderblade, and liver hanging on his horns – and hereby also hangs the conclusion to our tale from the *Tain*.

At each place that the bull dropped part of his conquest's body so that place was named. He dropped the shoulderblade and the place was called Finnlethe, the white one's shoulderblade. He dropped the liver and so Tromma was named. He tore up the ground at Cuib to give us Gort mBuraig, the Field of the Trench. And between times he stooped and discarded the loins and so Ath Luan, the Ford of the Loins, was named.

The Irish desire to have a legend for each place name knows no bounds. During the great battle for the bulls Maeve was caught by a very womanly affliction and knelt to relieve herself. Perhaps the scribes have the last laugh for, as Thomas Kinsella tells us:

Then Medb got her gush of blood.

"Fergus," she said, "take over the shelter of shields at the rear of the men of Ireland until I relieve myself."

"By God," Fergus said, "you have picked a bad time for this."

"I can't help it," Medb said. "I'll die if I can't do it."

And they called the place Fual Medba, Maeve's Foul Place.

Such are the tales and the tellers of tales we met on our voyages. There are others waiting your arrival. And there is more than history and myth and sights ancient and modern to delay the traveller. For the crew in search of leisure, who may hire a cruiser or bring their own craft up from Limerick or New Ross or along the Grand Canal from Dublin, there are regattas and fairs, angling competitions and wild stormy dances in marquees by the waterside. There are forgotten creeks to explore by dinghy and safe harbours in which to moor. And it is the tourist who will secure the future of this waterway, for without him there are simply not enough craft using the water to persuade the Government to spend money on its upkeep. The small but stoic Inland Waterways Association of Ireland, who did so much to help us throughout our voyage—and of which we are now proud members—have managed to maintain public interest in the Shannon as something more than just a convenient way of getting water to the turbines at Ardnacrusha.

Caution and common sense will get you anywhere on this waterway system and even the experienced skipper always remembers that he is cruising in inland seas capable of storm-force winds. Icebergs have been seen in the large lakes in winter. Keep to the main buoyed channel. (Admiralty Chart No 5078 for Lough Ree and No 5080 for Lough Derg are available although some hire companies forbid passage beyond the routes marked on their own charts.) Listen to the advice of the pierhead parliaments which assemble each evening on almost every quay.

Travel where you will—to Rooskey and Drumsna, Safe Harbour and Lecarrow, Banagher and Shannon Bridge. Head your bows into the Carranadoe Waters which lie to the west of the main river just south of Carrick. Many a boat has turned in there to make a brief visit to those isolated narrows and not been seen again for a week. The crew was not lost They had fallen under that Shannon spell which echoes Ireland's motto for the traveller—the land of time enough.

TWO

The Road from Dublin

WE HAVE ALWAYS had to disembark from the overnight Liverpool ferry at seven a.m. and, grown wise to the failures of Dublin's early morning haute cuisine, we usually spend an hour or so walking along the banks of the Grand Canal which makes a delightful linear park through the city. Then to Bewley's Oriental Café in Grafton Street or Westmoreland Street, where everything is dark wood and tiles and well polished. Even the waitresses, in neat maroon pinafores, who offer you a choice between Indian and China tea, are scrubbed for the occasion. You can sit at a private velvet-cushioned booth, which has changed little since the establishments were founded in the nineteenth century, and watch the regulars assemble beneath the stained-glass windows and steaming urns.

It is in Bewley's that our boiled egg arrives timed to the minute of our request, the toast is hot and the marmalade vintage. And then, to top off this sumptuous repast, we devour the first of many Irish sticky buns; not an Irish whiskey bun as the printer's gremlin once had it. Bewley's is the true gateway to Ireland, a sea of tranquillity in the mad babble of Dublin traffic. Joshua Bewley set up his first shop near Dame Street in the early 1840s and contented himself in selling tea, sugar and a little coffee until his son Ernest expanded the business. Following a row with a relative who used to supply the coffee, Ernest purchased a hundredweight of the precious bean from another supplier and set about converting the bourgeoisie to the new liquor. He held demonstrations and provided home-made rolls. Such was the genesis of the first Oriental Café, so called because Ernest also sold oriental ornaments. By 1903 a herd of Jersey cows had been imported and to this day the shops are supplied with milk and fresh eggs from the home farm at Moyvalley in County Kildare.

Bewley's is more than an eating house; it is a way of life, both for the regular customers and the staff. The organisation is a trust and any member of staff with more than three years' service may become a member of the Bewley Community which, among its articles, holds that it will encourage "thinking in terms of the welfare of the community in which we live, rather than a desire for personal gain at the cost of others". High sentiments for a restaurant. The commandments continue: "Many of the evils which threaten the world arise from 'a desire for personal gain at the cost of others'. The changes which have been made in the company are intended as our joint contribution towards a better world " Having eaten there we would say that the contribution is priceless.

It is time to set off on the road to Carrick on Shannon. It is not one of Ireland's most scenic routes and it was astonishing how different the landscape was to appear some weeks later when we retraced our steps, passing a little to the south by boat on the Grand Canal. Through Maynooth, Mullingar and Longford we drove until, just past Newtown Forbes, we caught sight of the first Shannon lake of our trip, Lough Forbes. We went northwards to Rooskey where the road runs beside the river and then headed inland again with brief glimpses of Loughs Bofin and Boderg until we arrived at the villages of Drumsna and Jamestown. At each of these a bridge carries the road across the Shannon which executes a sharp U-turn, bypassed for navigation by the Jamestown canal. Once over Jamestown bridge we were soon at the outskirts of Carrick, and went in search of the poet's "Lovely Bush Hotel".

> Through foreign climes I've wandered
>   And seen some princely domes,
> In Belfast and in Dublin fair
>   There are some splendid homes;

But in countries grand or cities great
   No building can excel
That mansion grand in Carrick town
   The Lovely Bush Hotel.

In the centre of the town it stands,
   Beside the chapel high
Where pious people pray to Him
   Who rules the earth and sky,
And daily hear in tones so clear
   The voice of Christian bell,
Which sounds as sweet as music, through
   The Lovely Bush Hotel.

I've seen the lovely bush from which
   The building takes its name;
It grew so grand beside the door,
   And likewise grew in fame;
Till one bright day 'twas cut away,
   But then it never fell—
For its name and fame will always live
   In the Lovely Bush Hotel.

Our anonymous bard hardly does the place justice but although the building's architectural merits do not justify the term mansion it is certainly the largest hotel in the town. We were welcomed by Tom Maher whose family have been established there for six generations. The present building was constructed in 1900 with later additions in 1969 and the walls of the lobby and passageways are lined with memorabilia of the days when the Bush had "Posting in all its Branches" and "bus and car attended the arrival and departure of all trains". The latter service was no doubt inaugurated because the railway station lies a mile out of town on the opposite bank of the river. Such was the popularity of Carrick at the turn of the century, although one suspects that even then the bustle of the place was mainly due to its position midway between the two coasts, that the original thatched house was demolished. Tom's grandmother, Ellen Mac Dermott, was keen to retain her licence during rebuilding and her letter asking to move to temporary premises is interesting in view of the temporary venue.

To His Excellency Earl Cadogan, K.C.
Lord Lieutenant General and General Governor of Ireland,
The Memorial of Ellen MacDermott, of Carrick on Shannon,
Hotel Keeper and Publican, widow.
Humbly Showeth: —
That Memorialist is throwing her house — which is a thatched one — and is about building a larger concern and slating it, in order to meet the requirements of the tourist traffic which is increasing for the last three years.
That Memorialist respectfully requests your Excellency under the circumstances will grant her a temporary transfer of her bar to a suitable house and premises in the Main Street — known as the Temperance Hotel formerly — which she has taken for the purpose of carrying on the hotel business say for twelve months or until such time as the new premises are completed.
It is, your Memorialist believes, in your Excellency's prerogative, to grant this permission and if your Excellency is pleased to comply, Memorialist will, as in duty bound, ever pray.
Bush Hotel,
Carrick on Shannon,
30th October, 1900.

The Earl was more interested in tax from excisable liquor than the Temperance Movement and he granted the transfer by return of post. A good deal quicker, said Tom, than such a thing would be organised today. In December 1902 the new premises were insured by the Alliance Assurance Company for £2,030 at a premium of £5 1s 6d, this to include the milk cows, piggery, slaughterhouse, hide house and bacon house. All these have gone, though Tom still farms twenty acres. Guests may dine well and Clew Bay oysters and Guinness topped our own dinner menu in the dining-room which overlooks the water.
Carrick on Shannon lies in County Leitrim and is the smallest

county town in Ireland. The signpost on your approach reads Carra Droma Ruisc, the weir of the marshy ridge, for although Carrick generally derives from the Irish *carraig*, a rock, here it is a corruption of *carra*, a weir. The town's present importance is still bound up with the river for the largest number of hire cruisers are based here.

We have always noticed the neatness of Carrick, which seemed to indicate a special pride among the inhabitants, and our thoughts were confirmed when Tom emerged from his office clutching a tiny local guide, *Picturesque Carrick on Shannon*. Produced before the Second World War the booklet was compiled by the local postmaster. This copy belonged to Tom's mother and since it is now out of print and a valuable rarity in the town, we were only able to browse through it while we remained in the hotel. It is a dotty little volume, full of the minutiae of country-town life with details of everything from cattle fairs to bus and train time-tables. It concludes with a chapter titled "Cleanliness", in which the author, J. J. Sheerin, trips over himself with superlatives about his native town.

Still another attraction which Carrick on Shannon possesses (and it is one which most visitors appreciate) is the cleanliness of its streets and the bright, attractive, and inviting appearance presented by its house fronts, particularly those of the hotels and principal shops. The windows are cleaned regularly and paint is used freely on the doors and other woodwork when required. This has always been a noticeable characteristic of Leitrim's capital.

With friends like that one wonders if the town of Carrick has ever needed Bord Fáilte Eireann, the Irish Tourist Board, to promote its pleasures.

Our boat was not to be ready until the following afternoon. We had previously visited the northern limits of the Shannon and its tributary the Boyle by water and decided to spend some hours revisiting this area by car. I particularly wanted to discover how work was progressing on the opening of the Lough Allen Canal. We stopped first at Leitrim, where Carthy's Bar lies beside the bridge

A sheltered anchorage in Lough Key at the foot of the Curlew Mountains, the northernmost limit of navigation

Carraig Locha Cé, the rock of Lough Key with MacDermott's castle and memories of the sad romance of Una Bhan.

The boatyard with welcome moorings at Portaneena on the Inner Lakes of Lough Ree.

Lively weather for the Shannon One Design Championships on Lough Ree.

and quay which mark the entrance to the Ballinamore and Bally-connell navigation. Carthy's is a darkly wooded, old-fashioned Irish bar, and it was with amazement, as our eyes grew accustomed to the gloom, that we spied an enormous pool table in the centre of the room. American pool, I exclaimed, only to be rebuked by the information that this was Irish-American pool and sure enough there was a label on the table to that effect. Whatever you call it I still wonder how the players can see the tips of their cues in this place. The appearance of these tables is certainly more welcome than the massive colour television sets which have invaded many once quiet hostelries to turn convivial meeting places into shrines, with the cathode ray as an altar.

Behind Carthy's, running along the course of what was, before the canal was built, the Leitrim River, is the Fair Field, which is being landscaped and provided with waterside seats. I hope that a few decent moorings are included, since the quay outside the bar sports a mighty underwater rock on which more than one cruiser has had a sticky moment. The conversation in Carthy's that day concerned a Gardai raid on a nearby village where the bars should have been shut on the occasion of Good Friday. This is a very strange state of affairs in Ireland and when the Garda entered the first bar he was not surprised to find it doing business as usual. Being a diligent man, and also recognising that he was outnumbered, he set off to the barracks for assistance. On his return the place was empty, as was every other bar nearby. Now that is a novel and honest way in which to enforce the law. "To be found open on Good Friday would cost a great deal more than to be found open after hours at any other time of the year," announced the lady who was drawing my pint. We all nodded in agreement. "There are," she continued, "a great many things which none of us will ever understand about the law." We all nodded to that too.

Having confirmed that the quality of Carthy's stout was as it should be we drove on to the tiny village of Battlebridge where even the bar is derelict. From there we went up the line of the Lough Allen Canal. Although the channel had been dredged the lock gates had still to be installed. The Office of Public Works later confirmed that work would be finished in 1977.

3

On we went, by a charming series of twisting country roads, to the State-owned forest park on the shores of Lough Key which includes the demesne of Rockingham. The house which stood here was built by John Nash in the first decade of the nineteenth century, but was later altered by Robert King, the first Lord Lorton, on the whim that another Nash house in Ireland was of grander proportions. The house was gutted by fire in 1863, rebuilt and destroyed again by fire in 1957. Today nothing remains of what has been variously described as "the best example of a Nash country house" and "a top-heavy mausoleum in a green graveyard". The latter description would appear to better reflect the "improvements" which its owner carried out, but even this could have been nothing to the monstrosity which now occupied the site. Beside a gaping hole which once contained the cellars there rises a concrete observation tower. It is a most intrusive form of modern tourism, ridiculous in the extreme since it plunders the very view which it invites you to its summit to scan. Climb to a nearby hill and the view will unfold itself just as easily.

Apart from this monument to modern man's insensitivity to landscape the park at Rockingham is a handsome sight, with wide views across the lake to a mountain backdrop. The green-backed islands, one for every county in the land runs the tale, dimple the blue-black waters of the lake and on a still day it is easy to imagine that you are gazing at some architect's painted papier maché image of his ideal creation. From the grassy knoll on which the house stood we descended a cobbled tunnel running to the water's edge. Antechambers led off this subterranean walk and in one of these, from which came the sound of dripping water, lay a large wooden wheel and a circular ridged walk. It may well have housed some form of horse-drawn water pump, for the house was so constructed that a number of these damp and gloomy passageways led to the underground servant's quarters.

The principle of Nash's design, although he built on the site of an earlier house and may have incorporated an older cellar area, was to construct the ultimate tradesman's entrance. No scullion or labourer was to sully the view of the lakes and gardens from the windows of Rockingham and so, as the servants toiled in their dungeon, the proud owners strutted the tonsured lawns above their heads. Beneath stairs took on a new meaning on this estate.

The tenants of Rockingham fared little better than the servants and we later heard an horrific account of their treatment. At the time of the evictions in the mid-nineteenth century many small farmers on the estate rebelled. They were rounded up and punished for the defence of their homes. There was no trial. The punishment was not just harsh, but obscene in its conception, and gives some idea of the way in which the Anglo-Irish viewed the native stock as little more than animals. The offenders were forced to carry panniers of manure until their backs bled from contact with the rough containers and the muck worked its way into their wounds. Then they were flogged and imprisoned for a day without food.

Like many old-established Anglo-Irish families the tree of the Kings, who came to Connacht with Sir Richard Bingham during the Elizabethan wars, is as complicated as their allegiances are many. Around 1663, three years after the restoration of Charles II and the modification of Cromwell's Act of Settlement, the King brothers, Baron Kingston and Sir Robert, were awarded lands. Although the Baron, then Sir John King, had been an ardent Cromwellian, he had been wise enough to change to the Royalist cause. The fortunes of the family were split, rival factions established, and when they were not fighting on some battlefield they were locked in a long series of court actions over the ownership of the many estates to which, of course, they had no moral title. In 1805 Robert Edward King, Baron Erris of Boyle, brother of the Earl of Kingston, was created a Viscount and he took the title Lorton from a local place name.

The family history is almost too bizarre to be believed. In 1824 the Earl of Kingston tried to sell family lands in Sligo and the débâcle which ensued between the brothers took fifteen years to pass through the courts, in the course of which Lord Kingston was proclaimed insane. The House of Lords found in favour of Lord Lorton in 1839, and his rule of the tenantry was vigorous.

In the late 1830s a Father Mathew became Ireland's Apostle of Temperance, riding through the country at the head of a crusade. When he arrived in Limerick one Sunday in November 1839 it was reported that "ten thousand persons knelt upon the pavement and solemnly vowed never again to touch the poison of their race". By the Shannon quay he received the pledges of seven hundred fishermen and the performance continued in the streets, the churches, and even the courthouse until Father Mathew's "voice failed him and he could no longer repeat the words". Making his way up the Shannon the priest arrived in Boyle and it is not surprising that the workers of the Rockingham estate should wish to see this famous figure. Lord Lorton might have been expected to see an advantage in the greater sobriety of his workers. But idleness, and listening to a priest was the wont of an idle man according to Lord Lorton, would appear to have been a greater vice than drink. The men were "exhorted and enjoined to attend to their harvest work". Daniel O'Connell had a few scathing words to say about his "saintly lordship" when he heard of the affair.

Not every inhabitant of the estate left such cruel memories. I discovered in the *Annals of Rockingham*, a modern history published by the *Roscommon Herald* in 1959, a copy of which was presented to us by Tom Maher, that in the 1630s Edward, the fourth son of Sir John King, was drowned at the age of twenty-five. Below the title of Milton's pastoral elegy *Lycidas* is written: "In the Monody the Author bewails a learned Friend, unfortunately drown'd in his Passage from Chester on the Irish Seas, 1637." The friend, on his way to Dublin, was Edward King, Cambridge scholar, for whom a memorial volume of verse was collected and in which *Lycidas* first appeared.

> He must no flote upon his watry bear
> Unwept, and welter to the parching wind
> Without the meed of som melodious tear.

At the beginning of the twentieth century Balfour's policy of killing Home Rule with kindness was well under way and Rockingham played its part in land reform, as this account, from the columns of the *Roscommon Herald*, shows:

Lord Dudley, Lord Lieutenant of Ireland, then had his

residence in Rockingham and both he and Lady Dudley were determined to use their influence to settle the land question in Ireland. Bringing the Chancellor of the Exchequer in the English House of Commons on a visit to Rockingham seemed the best method to soften his heart and so entice him to provide the necessary money for the land purchase. Lavishly entertained in Rockingham Lady Dudley took her illustrious guest on a trip by the north of Loch Key, over the Curlews and back by the slums of Boyle. She had carefully arranged with the coachman that whenever a really squalid house and barefooted hungry children appeared he was to drive slowly but when things looked better he was to whip up his horses. When the Chancellor returned to England he reported that he had seen only two good houses in Ireland, Rockingham House and the Vice-Regal Lodge. And so Ireland got the Wyndham Act in 1903; with one hundred million pounds to buy out the landlords.

In 1959, on the sale of the demesne which had remained with the family after the Land Act had denuded it of the tenanted section, the local newspaper wrote its own epitaph. It is as true and telling as anything Milton wrote in *Lycidas*: "And there in sombre silence we left all that remains of a day and age that will never return." Today the babble of children's voices can be heard in the grounds, yachts and cruisers moor in the elegant stone harbour, and a gentleman's paradise has been gently transformed into a vast public playground. But nothing, except that tower, has been allowed to interfere with the original features.

We were told that the camping and caravan site was not opened until a shelter belt of trees and shrubs made it almost invisible. The reception building, with charts of the nature trails, and the restaurant are built of a dark wood which blends into the environment. There is plenty of evidence of the ability of those early gardeners to adapt, rather than batter, nature into some kind of order as you stroll along the beech walk to the astounding gate-house which actually straddles the road. A riot of exotic flowering shrubs, imported to enhance the natural growth, still swamp the air with a heady bouquet. Canals cut through the greensward, constructed not only to provide boat channels so that turf might be brought to the entrance of the underground tunnel, but also to make sheltered creeks for all manner of water-loving plants and birds. One of these canals is spanned by the Fairy Bridge, built of stone dredged from the lake bed. There was not a leprechaun in sight, although we would have been little surprised to have met a brownie cavorting in this magic place.

Before we leave this pastoral spot there is one old story of the lake which I have to tell. It comes from the misty times before the Kings and Rockingham, when this land was the ancestral seat of the Mac Dermotts. The English were not the first to take what was not theirs. This Irish family had wrested control from an earlier clan, the Mac Greeveys.

According to the legend the Mac Dermott who lived on the island, known as Carraig Locha Cé, the rock of Lough Key, had a beautiful daughter, called Una Bhan. The girl fell in love with a local lad but Mac Dermott would not countenance the relationship and banished his daughter to her room. The girl pined for her lover and it was clear that she would die. Mac Dermott summoned the boy to her bedside but although she recovered he still refused to permit them to marry. The boy told Mac Dermott that he would wait one hour by the River Boyle. If the chieftain did not come to offer his daughter's hand he would cross the water and never return. When the time had run out the boy crossed the water only to hear the old chief galloping towards him pleading for his return. But the boy continued on his way and Una Bhan died in her cold and lonely tower. From then on the boy, overcome by the result of his pride, slept each night on her grave on Trinity Island. One day he was drowned. Mac Dermott buried him beside his daughter and they lie to this day out on Lough Key by the site of an old monastery. It is not for nothing that this seemingly dainty bowl of water is known in Irish as Loch Cé, the lake of the night.

THREE

On the Waterfront

OUR FRIENDS IN IRELAND tell us that if you can see the mountains it is about to rain and that if you cannot see the mountains it is already raining. As we made our way down to the jetty at Carrick there was not a mountain in sight and despite the reassurances of Eugene Gibney, who manages the boat station, that the soft Leitrim rain would in no way spoil our departure we were decidedly damp as we loaded everything from the library to the kitchen sink on board *Fenniscourt Star*. It was the last rain we were to encounter for three weeks but it was roundly cursed at the time, even if it does provide greener grass, much loved by cows and photographers.

We were anxious to be away and Eugene came on board to explain the purpose of the various lights, buzzers, dials, switches and levers on the control console. This done he cast off our warps and the voyage had begun. We slipped slowly down river beneath the bridge, mindful of our wash since there was a number of fours and eights about. Once into Lough Corry I was able to open up the 72 HP Perkins diesel and with a thunderous roar *Fenniscourt* lifted her bows and showed her paces on open water. We spent some time manœuvring around imaginary obstacles which must have been a source of some amusement to any landlubber on the bank. But it is always better to sense the handling characteristics of a new craft before meeting your first real obstacle, in this case the narrow starboard turn into Jamestown cut leading to the lock. Matty Burke was out to see us through.

On we went through Loughs Tap, Boderg and Boffin until we
entered the narrow river section leading past the village of Rooskey
and another lock. Neither Val, nor myself, was greatly interested
in the scenery at this point; we were too busy savouring the delights
of the boat. But as we passed south through Lough Forbes it was
all eyes to port as we searched for the entrance to the Camlin River.
The main course of the Shannon continues due south but by entering the Camlin there is a circular route which takes you back into
the main stream via another lock south of Tarmonbarry.

We had navigated this section before but even so we were upon
the reed-shrouded entrance, the navigation markers barely visible,
almost too late to make the turn. The Camlin is a delightful change
from the sweep of the wider Shannon. Here there is barely room for
two craft to pass and at some points the trees poised across the
water from both banks make such a passage quite impossible. The
river meanders in a series of ox-bows and another craft, seemingly
approaching, is often moving in the same direction on another loop.

As we moved into the lock below Richmond Harbour the rain
vanished and the sun clove its way into the suddenly cloudless sky.
Frank Martin, the lock-keeper, was there to help us through into
the basin which marks the terminus of the sadly derelict Royal
Canal, the Grand Canal's rival route from Dublin until its closure
shortly after the Second World War. Richmond Harbour, in the
tiny village of Cloondara, Cluain-da-Rath, the meadow of the two
forts, was a bustling port at the turn of the century. The warehouses, a flax mill, now converted into one of the village bars, and a
delightful row of colour-washed cottages flank the quay. Beyond
the harbour lie the flax fields, now pasture land. The village was not
always thus and it was the canal which led to its creation and brief
prosperity. A letter in the *Carrick Morning Post* in 1819 drew attention to "the misfortune of the Royal Canal, to have a most unsuitable
and incommodious termination". The writer bemoaned the fact that
the traveller in search of accommodation or refreshment "must
proceed near a mile along the Shannon, and cross the bridge of
Tarmonbarry to arrive at that inconsiderable little village, which is
situate on the west bank of the river". No doubt the limitations of
Tarmonbarry – Termonbarry is an alternative spelling – prompted

the establishment of no fewer than three hostelries on the opposite shore.

We set off up a road which led along the canal bank for a few hundred yards before branching away towards the Shannon. It was on this road that we came out on to the first high bog of our journey, the terrain ripped of its ground cover by the vast machines which now gather the turf. As the sun set across this wild desert-like place the bog changed colour from russet to bloody crimson. It was a fantastic light which seemed even to stop the birds in the hedgerows in mid-song as we strolled back to Fenniscourt for supper in that sudden chill which follows the fallen sun on a warm evening.

After supper we adjourned to Mr. Croghan's bar which lies on the island formed by the canal and the River Fallan which flow side by side through the village. It was, as we had been assured by Frank, a fine and comfortable place. But the first night out of port is always the most dangerous. Let us say that Mr. Croghan's pints were too grand and my seat far too comfortable. Before that point where inebriation outweighs conversation and everyone has to resort to singing, we managed to learn something of the waterway from Frank. The Camlin route was the original passage, having been constructed in 1776. Since it was the two-hundredth anniversary of Frank's lock a celebration round was called for. Before the barges were motor-driven progress along the Camlin, too narrow and twisting for the use of sail, was achieved by punting the barges. Two men walked the length of each boat with their poles firmly lodged in the mud. It must have been a laborious passage.

The following morning I walked over to the home of the Tarmonbarry lock-keeper, John Burke. John's lock on the main river was constructed in the 1840s but he lives in a cottage beside the lock which leads into the Shannon from the Camlin route. The Shannon Commissioners closed this route when the new lock was built but they saved themselves the expense of a new lock house. The old lock was repaired some years ago when Richmond Harbour was dredged to provide the increasing number of pleasure craft with a safe mooring. John has worked on the Shannon for more than thirty years but do not enquire as to his duties or he will simply reply that he is "doing as little as ever before". We sat round the enormous hissing turf-fired range—fully stoked in spite of the bright sunshine outside—and yarned awhile until the sound of *Fenniscourt*'s horn summoned me back for lunch.

It was a balmy moonlit night at Lanesborough, our next port of call, just right for an open-air party which was just as well since the makings of one arrived as three cruisers berthed and disgorged thirty or so employees of the Royal Dublin Show who had been spending a riotous weekend on the river. Would we care to share the vin du pays and contribute a tune to their carousings? It has always been my belief in such cases that if you can't beat them, join them. And so we did, and the sun was rousing the night from its slumbers as we pitched wearily into our bunks.

Since time immemorial Ireland has made use of the great boglands which stretch across the hinterland. In 1948 Bord na Mona was established by the Government to provide a turf fuel source for the Electricity Supply Board's generating stations. In spite of this long history of turf use, Ireland was not the first nation to embark on such a scheme; that distinction goes to the USSR. Germany also makes use of this fuel and much of the machinery used in Ireland is imported from there.

Having arranged from London to be conducted round, we were soon being ushered through the great cavern of the power station by Michael Malone, who must be one of the Board's most enthusiastic employees. No nook or cranny was omitted from our tour and we circled round the ground-floor furnaces—of enormous proportions due to the poor quality of the fuel which contains a great deal of water—and then climbed several hundred feet up iron ladders and across narrow catwalks to the top of the building where we came across the great open maw of the hopper which stores the turf to be fed to the flames. While Michael was reeling off facts and figures about megawatts, cycles, boilers, condensers and revolutions, breaking off for a brief moment to point out the splendid view of the river to be had at such a height, I remained with my eyes tightly closed, grasping a handrail for support. Was there, I pleaded, a lift to convey us to ground level. There was, announced

Michael with pleasure. There was also a box full of heavy weights on the floor of the elevator which I was told, as we plummeted earthwards, was to stop the cage shooting through the roof. I did not discover what happened when it hit the basement as we stopped at the ground-floor level. For that Michael will forever have my gratitude.

It was with the greatest difficulty that we persuaded him that there was no need for us to go inside the boiler. It was, he pointed out, shut down or on "hold off" as they call it. From the way he attempted to encourage us to enter the bowels of this monster you would have thought that the entire station had come to a standstill just to allow two visitors to enter it.

We left Michael to his boilers and bunkers and quotas and consumptions and passed out of the throbbing din into a glorious May morning. On our way back to *Fenniscourt* for lunch we saw one of the great and ever-growing hazards of turf-fired power stations. The fine ash created by the furnaces is dumped in a great bank, rather curiously called an ash pond. The ash contains sulphur which is poisonous to fish and although the main flow of the river here is on the opposite bank, the pond looked perilously close to the water. The ash is also passed into the air from the stack, although ESB officials assured us that as a result of complaints from the town — Monday washday being more of an ash Wednesday when the wind was in the right direction — a system of fans had been installed which arrested the ash before it could make its way into the air. Back at the harbour we wondered just how effective the fans were since *Fenniscourt* lay under a layer of fine grey dust.

After lunch we walked out to the rail terminal where Tom McGrath met us with a small railcar. Tom sat in the middle facing sideways and could thus propel us in any direction we wished to go. Switching on the V 8 engine we were soon banging and swaying along the most unparallel set of rails I have had the misfortune to see. "There's one man on permanent way duty all the time but we get derailments quite often," said Tom, in reply to the rather worried look on both our faces. And sore backsides too, I thought, as we bucketed apparently springless across the gaps between sections.

There is more than eighty miles of narrow gauge track along

which trucks, pulled by Leeds-built Wagon Master diesel loco-motives, deliver fuel to the power station. As we approached the bridge which carries the trains across the Shannon, Tom slowed to a crawl. Once across we continued our pitching way along the main line and arrived at the great machine which actually cuts the peat sods. As we clambered out of the railcar and sank to our ankles, Tom reassured us with the information that only a few weeks ago a tractor would have sunk out of sight if it had tried to cross the bog. The peat-cutting machine is definitely one for the Heath Robinson gallery. At one end cutters slice into the high bank and then the sods travel along a conveyor belt which runs out from the machine across the wide trench already cut. Every few seconds the sods are dumped in a line several hundred feet long and are left to dry before stacking, further drying, and eventual transport to the furnaces. What stops you in your tracks, apart from being ankle-deep in powdery bog, is that the machine, for all its size, is almost silent. Night and day without halt this mammoth drags ponderously across the landscape, powered from the station by the very turf it cuts. All along the line of the bog are vast sockets. Plug her in and away you go.

This method has been largely overtaken by the use of milled peat, a far less spectacular process and one not much loved by Shannon boaters. On Derryaroge Bog the area is laid out in a series of fifty feet wide drying fields, the surface of which is cut by a machine pulling a spiked drum. The milled peat is harrowed to accelerate drying, scraped into ridges and then carried away in wagons. The fine particles which result are caught by the smallest breath of wind and can quickly silt up any nearby river.

Three hundred thousand tons of milled peat are harvested from the bogs surrounding Lanesborough each year with a further one hundred and ten thousand tons of sod peat. Ireland's total pro-duction is an enormous three million tons of milled and one million tons of sod peat annually. Among Bord na Mona's other products are peat briquettes, dried and compressed blocks of turf which have taken over in many areas from the traditionally hand-cut variety. And then there is the Irish moss peat so greatly loved by gardeners throughout the world. This comes from two bogs in County Kildare

where the turf is light, fibrous and mainly sphagnum in origin.
While at Lanesborough we had become friends with two young
lads from the town and that evening the four of us, not forgetting
their dog Nipper – because he does – set off south into Lough Ree
for a visit to Quaker Island which lay seven miles distant. Dennis
and Francis said their parents were quite happy to let them come
with us – apparently half the town had observed our journey across
the bog in what is grandly known as the "Director's Car". Anyone
who uses this élite vehicle passes some sort of respectability test.
We discovered later that half the town also thought that anyone
using the bog railway was quite insane. Since this confidence was
imparted by a local gentleman who was buying me a pint of stout at
the time I was quite unable to disagree.

There was a lively breeze from the east as we nosed up to the
mooring buoy in the wide unsheltered bay of Inis Clothrann, as
Quaker Island is more properly called. It also manages to be
stamped Inchcleraun in the Ordnance Survey map. Val and the
boys set off in the dinghy while I remained behind in case the
weather should worsen.

The Island of Clothra, Queen Maeve's sister, is as steeped in
folklore as any place associated with this Irish Boadicea. St. Diarmid
established a religious settlement here in the sixth century and the
remains of six churches still stand, though these are probably of a
later date. Stepping on to the island is like being transported by
Tardis. Faint paths lead you through a shelter belt of trees and
bushes to the sacred glades and hollows, but you are unlikely to
see another human being. You may wander at will through the
ruins and my favourite is the tiny Teampall Dhiarmada. It is only
around eight foot square and must be the smallest place of worship
in Ireland. But the names of the churches are all equal in their
magic – Teampall Mor, the Great Church, Teampall Mhuire,
St. Mary's Church, and the fearful Teampall na Marbh, the
Church of the Dead. How much better they sound in Irish!

Inis Clothrann is not the kind of place where I would like to
spend a night alone. It is to here, they say, that Queen Maeve
retreated after the death of her husband and it is here, at Grianan
Meidhbe, that she is said to have bathed and met her end by the

hand of Forbaith, son of the King of Ulster. We were nearing the
end of the story which John Weaving had begun for us. Maeve's
followers took the body away to the top of the mountain called
Knocknarea. The men of Ireland came to throw stones on the
cairn and so constructed the largest monument in the land. It is
called Miosgan Meabha, which rather lamely translates as Maeve's
Lump. It rises to thirty-four feet and has a circumference of 200 feet.

Centuries later another Irish poet was to seek inspiration for his
muse from the spirits of ancient Ireland, the *sidhe*. Queene Maeve
and her hosts lived again in Yeats' *The Hosting of The Sidhe*, first
published in 1899;

> The host is rising from Knocknarea
> And over the grave of Clooth-na-Bare;
> Caoilte tossing his burning hair,
> And Niamh calling *Away, come away;*
> *Empty your heart of its mortal dream.*
> *The winds awaken, the leaves whirl round,*
> *Our cheeks are pale, our hair is unbound,*
> *Our breasts are heaving, our eyes are agleam,*
> *Our arms are waving, our lips are apart,*
> *And if any gaze on our rushing band,*
> *We come between him and the deed of his hand,*
> *We come between him and the hope of his heart.*
> The host is rushing 'twixt night and day,
> And where is there hope or deed as fair?
> Caoilte tossing his burning hair,
> And Niamh calling *Away, come away.*

The legends live on in contemporary verse and song. And new
legends are made, for how did this place ever come to be known as
Quaker Island? There is a curious story, collected by Mary Banim
during her tour in the late nineteenth century, which tells of strange
creatures in the lake and of a banshee who still wails on the shore
where Maeve died. The banshee, Miss Banim tells us, was responsible for the island farmer's discovery of the body of a drowned
youth on the island shore. The farmer, Mr. O'Farrell, appears to

have been a very talkative fellow and this is one of the stories he
told.

You saw the Quaker gentleman's empty house below? Very
well. When that gentleman came to build that cottage nothing in
the world would do him but to pitch on the finest stones in the
Clogas Church for the keystones of his summer house. He yoked
his horses to the first stone to draw it down, when—as sure as
I'm speaking to you—the cattle went raging mad and tore across
the island in such a fury they had to be shot. And not that alone,
but every living creature on the island—save the Christians—
went mad too, and never was seen such consternation, until
Mr. Fairbrother vowed a solemn vow he'd never touch another
stone from any one of the holy churches. Then the creatures got
back their peace.

Miss Banim's sage was too wise to believe all the tales of his
island home. He warned of the perils of entering the cloister beside
the Virgin's Church. Any woman who did so would die within the
twelvemonth. But a widow did enter at the funeral of her husband,
said Mr. O'Farrell.

Sure as day, the ground opened and swallowed her but after
a time she was resurrected out of the ground again, beyond there,
just behind my house. They do say there's an underground
passage from the old Lis to the churches. The earth swallowed
her in the forbidden ground, and it wouldn't have happened if
she wasn't here, so that argument does not alter the case, save
and except that she didn't die all out.

Reading that passage Val and I began to learn how the stuff of
legends is sown.
Coming on deck I discovered that Val and the boys were having
some trouble getting away from the shore. The flat-bottomed
dinghy was being blown back on to the rocky beach between each
stroke of the oars. Eventually, with the boys in the water to their
waist and jumping on at the last moment, Val made it through the

shoreline breakers and pulled for *Fenniscourt*. Progress was slow but by letting out the mooring rope attached to the buoy and then casting a line to the dinghy I thought I might be able to heave them alongside. The mooring-rope operation went well enough but each time I cast the rope it seemed to arrive at the wrong point. After a good deal of shouted oaths from Val about throwing bunches of knitting I eventually made contact. It was a sodden crew that made their way back to Lanesborough that night. Dennis and Francis thought the whole affair a splendid hoot. No doubt there are new legends about Quaker Island being told in Lanesborough School today.

There is little to interest the visitor in Lanesborough itself, although it is worth noting the concrete bridge which appears to have been built directly on top of a much older structure – if only as a warning of what not to do to old bridges. A feature of the town is that it consists of two parishes in two different dioceses in two counties in two provinces. The river is the dividing line. By straddling the centre of the bridge you will have one foot in County Longford in the Province of Leinster and the other in County Roscommon in the Province of Connacht. None of which is much reason for visiting a town.

We had been told to visit Vinny Farrell, who lives in the parish of Ballyleague on the eastern shore, and that evening we arrived at his door and were welcomed in like long-lost cousins. We got to talking about the changes which had taken place in Lanesborough and suddenly Vinny announced that the place was just like London. I felt the parallel rather exaggerated. Vinny would have none of it. "People here are so busy now," he said, "that they have little enough time to spend the time of day with you in the street." At least Vinny had time to spend the night with us.

He is a great man for the river and when Córas Iompair Eireann, the Irish state transport authority, sold the last of their cargo barges from the Dublin–Limerick run Vinny was to be found at the helm of a barge which had been purchased by a friend. It was a moving tale he told of those last voyages after which few of the barges would ever again pass through the Grand Canal.

"The people along the banks of the canal – workers, bank rangers

St. Ciaran's city fair, the holy settlement of Clonmacnois on the river section between Loughs Ree and Derg.

The harbour in Dromineer Bay, County Tipperary, with its sixteenth-century castle backdrop.

Stone-built harbour of Garrykennedy on Lough Derg which greatly resembles many of the fishing harbours in the south of England.

The inland sea of Lough Derg shows its teeth. Parker Point lies in the middle distance beyond which is the entrance to the arm of the lake leading to Killaloe.

and lock-keepers and their wives and children – would rush along the line after us to watch and to help the end of the boats. There were tears in the women's eyes and a good many of the lads were crying openly too. It wasn't tears of anger at the thought of losing their jobs but a real sadness as they knew it was the end of a way of life. Not everyone's way perhaps, but it was their way. And you know, they would come on board and tinker with the old Bolinder engine. There wasn't a thing I didn't know about those engines but it was more than I could do to interfere. They just wanted to help, to be there at the last."

Vinny of the Nine Lives, as his wife has dubbed him, has had many an adventure on the Shannon. Once his barge was blown on to the notorious Hagan Rock in Lough Derg. A storm broke and Vinny spent a fitful night being swept off and on the rock to which he had managed to secure the anchor. "The most unholy depression comes over a man in such a situation." The depression appears to have been caused by a lack of cigarettes. "I contemplated cutting the anchor rope but the wind was in the wrong direction to blow me to the shore. Then there was the sea-cock. But the brute kept swinging into deep water and I could never be sure that I would settle on the shallows round the rock. I was certain my ninth life was up when one of the CIE steamers still working at the time hove into view and put a line on board. The bloody barge is still cruising up and down the lough but I can tell you the name of one man who never steps on board."

FOUR

The Rising of the Moon

OUR RESPECT FOR the Shannon grew as a result of Vinny's cautionary tales. But the following morning was set fair as we nosed out of Lanesborough Harbour for the last time, passed south beneath the bridge, and headed down the lake by tree girt Inch MacDermot, Incheangh and Clawinish to our favourite Lough Ree mooring, Barley Harbour. Val kept her eye to the glasses as we left the buoyed channel and slipped to the east of the treacherous Iskeraulin Shoal, a needle-sharp reef hardly visible at low summer water levels. On this occasion a line of gulls, perched on the miniature peaks, marked the hazard clearly.

Barley Harbour was constructed by the local council in a fit of developmental enthusiasm which was not matched by their under-standing of the sailor's needs. While the gently rounded brown stone walls of the quay, backed by neat lawns and dry stone walls, are a delight to the eye the stunted trees, which were planted during the landscaping, bear witness to the exposed position. A rocky shoreline and a breakwater which ends before it can provide any real shelter make the site suitable only for fair weather mooring. But it is worth a detour, even if a change in the weather calls for a hasty exit. Here, by Leveret Point, in the pleasantly named township of Summersit, we were near the spot where the King of Ulster's son stood with his sling to cast his stone a full mile across the water and kill Queen Maeve. A handful of modern summer homes, stone faced with high-pitched slate roofs, peep from the trees and rhododendrons by the site of an older, smaller harbour. In summer the harbour is a popular picnic spot for local families and more often than not cars outnumber boats.

There is no village at Barley Harbour, but supplies are at hand. Along the road, lined with towering hedges of wild fuchsia and rose, is the home of a gentleman who owns a mobile grocery. You will catch him in the evening after he has finished his rounds and he will sell you fresh eggs, milk and bread along with a variety of tinned produce. He may, if you are lucky, agree to transport you in his van to the nearest inn, some five miles distant in Newtown Cashel. When we took up his offer he took the trouble to arrange for a friend who was enjoying a jar to convey us back to base, even if we did have to hold grimly to the back of a bucking tractor. The excursion is well worthwhile if only to see the bar emblazoned with a painted sign announcing that the proprietor, apart from selling groceries and animal foodstuffs, is also the provider of "all funeral requisites".

It was here in Barley Harbour, in a house built and furnished by his own hands, that we met Michael Casey, worker in wood. A year before we had chatted about his work and we had told him of a friend in Scotland who collected driftwood and fashioned it into abstract forms. We arrived once again at Michael's house and I had just got as far as saying that "you may not remember us, but . . ." when Michael declared that "sure, you're the man with a friend called David Morrison who makes pieces from the waves". And with that Michael led us into a rough gallery he has constructed, and there we saw his latest creations, great roots and sections of trees shaped by time and finished by the hand of this careful craftsman. These, however, did not come from any beach on Lough Ree but from the depths of the Irish bogs. Michael is a carver of bog wood.

It is an art he taught himself after many years as a carpenter building the imitation tinker caravans which are a popular holiday attraction in Ireland. It was not an easy craft to learn. First he had to persuade Bord na Mona to let him have the large pieces of wood which the machines which now rip the turf cast up from time to time. These had to be dried and stored for many years before he could start work. Today the workshop is lined with shelf upon shelf of drying rough-cut timber. On a shelf by the window stand the result of his labours. In spite of the mass of wood and shavings there is none of the fragrance of freshly-sawn wood since dead bog wood has no scent.

There are pieces as exquisite as anything you will see worked in precious metals. A wooden chalice, black as night, worked from bog oak; a simple desk pen holder and paper knife carved from bog yew, the depth of colour in the brown and auburn seams polished to life again after thousands of years in the pit of the bog and swamp lands. Michael's most recent work was a bookbinding in deal, with an elegant tracery and a leather spine and clasp. But the most finely wrought of his creations is a chess board, the border, squares and chess men worked by hand in contrasting bog timbers. When polished the lighter woods, such as yew and alder, give the impression of marble but with a softer hue. Anyone interested in an honest and well-made object to remind them of their visit to the Republic would do well to avoid the souvenir tat and visit Michael Casey at his Barley Harbour workshop. He supplies a number of shops in Dublin and other towns, and a cooperative craft centre in Strokestown, County Roscommon. But there is something about buying from the hands of the craftsman which makes the item more of a treasure.

But enough of this sales patter for our friend Michael. Later that day he came down to the quay and introduced us to the simple eloquence of another Casey, a poet who has been greatly over-shadowed by the works of Goldsmith whose association with these lands of the River Inny is known to every schoolchild in the land. Such is Goldsmith's fame that he has the distinction of being the only man to have his birthplace marked as such on the Ordnance Survey map. No such fame has followed the simple lyrics of John Keegan Casey whose family moved from Mount Dalton to Gorteen in 1854. Leo, as he was called to distinguish him from many other Caseys in the neighbourhood, was no Goldsmith as Michael is quick to agree but his muse was much in tune with the people, the pastures and the politics of this Shannonside landscape. But how many who today sing his best-known lyric, "The Rising of the

Moon" — to the tune of that equally well-known rebel song, "The
Wearing of the Green" — know anything of its author or the adapta-
tion he made to his own words? Here are the last three verses of
that stirring song:

> Out from many a mud wall cabin
> Eyes were watching thro' the night,
> Many a manly chest was throbbing
> For the blessed morning light.
> Murmurs passed along the valleys
> Like the banshee's lonely croon,
> And a thousand blades were flashing
> At the risin' of the moon.
>
> There beside the singing river
> That dark mass of men was seen,
> Far above the shining weapons
> Hung their own beloved green.
> "Death to every foe and traitor!
> Forward! strike the marchin' tune!
> And hurrah, my boys, for freedom!
> 'Tis the risin' of the moon."
>
> Well they fought for poor old Ireland,
> And full bitter was their fate,
> (Oh! what glorious pride and sorrow
> Fell the name of Ninety-eight.)
> Yet, thank God, e'en are beating
> Hearts in manhood's burning noon,
> Who should follow in their footsteps
> At the risin' of the moon.

"There beside the singing river," runs the song. But in the
original Casey had written, "There beside the Inny River". Thinking that the authorities might take the location literally and raid the
houses and farms that he loved the poet deleted the name of the
river.

Michael was intent to measure out the life and works of his favourite bard, and since we were also measuring out the Paddy — although Michael himself would only take a small cup of wine, and never before has such a small cup lasted such a long night — it seemed a good enough way in which to spend the evening. In 1866, with the publication of *A Wreath of Shamrocks*, Leo Casey became a celebrity in Ireland. His work fell into the hands of English critics and a writer in the *Saturday Review* commented that

> With all its taint of treason, it is not an unpleasant little work . . . Of course the Saxon comes in for it; but no Saxon could feel overvexed at being railed at so eloquently in his own language, and in a manner which demonstrates that the gentleman indulging in it must have been a sound student of the authors whose countrymen he curses as Kehema cursed.

England's tolerance for the young poet did not extend to his involvement in the secret society of the Fenian Brotherhood and he was sent to Mountjoy after the abortive rising of 1867. He was released and banished although he did not leave Ireland in the end since the authorities appear to have been more afraid of the effect of Casey's orations should he arrive in the United States, than of his poetic patriotism being read in his native land. Soon after his release he married Mary Josephine Briscoe and although the event was a tragic affair, with the best man arrested beforehand and the priest requiring a great deal of persuasion to tie the knot at all, the outcome had its moment of high humour. Casey knew that he was a marked man. He therefore decided that the safest place for the honeymoon would be in a boarding house in the shadow of Dublin Castle itself. Here the couple spent some happy days under the very noses of the Government spies. And they registered as Mr. and Mrs. Puritan Harrison.

Their union was short lived. After a public appearance at the St. Patrick's Day Mass in 1868 he was ignored by the authorities. The following year a Scottish publisher produced "The Rising of the Moon" but soon after, following an accident in a cab, he died. It is said that fifty thousand people followed his coffin to Glasnevin.

By the time Michael had exhausted his store of knowledge on Casey the moon was well risen and, leaving us with a beautiful edition of the poems, published in Dublin in 1878, he set off home promising that he had a rare treat in store for us the next afternoon.

The wind freshened during the night, but by moving all our fenders to one side and putting out a second stern line we were able to sleep safely. In the morning we took stock of the weather. There was still a stiff breeze from the shore but as there was no sign of heavy cloud we decided to attempt the short crossing to Safe Harbour, a tiny indentation on a peninsula which runs out from the Roscommon shore. The crossing to Rinnagan Point, clearly visible at the end of the dark line of St. John's Wood, was straightforward but as we turned to cross the mouth of St. John's Bay we came beam on to the sea. The harbour for which we were making offers no "safety" at all in easterly winds but since we did not intend to stay long, and certainly not overnight, we nosed slowly towards the anchorage and were relieved to see that a white mooring buoy had been laid. Catching mooring buoys while hanging over the pulpit of a wallowing boat is not Val's idea of fun and she was well baptised by the time she had the buoy on board and the bow line secure. Before departing in the dinghy I cast out the anchor as extra security since our stern was sweeping in an arc no more than a boat's length from the shore.

Making our way to the beach we could hardly distinguish, through the tangled forest, the great ruin of St. John's Castle, so called after the Hospital of St. John the Baptist whose members established a church near this spot. The narrow arm of land on which we were about to set foot is marked on both the Admiralty Chart – which dates from a survey made in 1837 and carries a warning that it has not been updated since then and should be used with "caution" – and the Ordnance Survey map as Warren Point, but it is better known as Rindoon, from the Irish Rinn Dún of Duin, the point of the fort. This is another example of topographical chaos caused by the decision to anglicise the original Irish place names. This transliteration reached its most ridiculous lengths when the original Irish "loch" was rewritten as "lough". As every Celt knows

few Englishmen can be bothered to get their tongues round the
"ch" sound and I was greatly amused one evening to hear the
modern consequence of this alleged sophistication. An English
visitor was busy describing the beauties of Lough Derg, but he
managed to pronounce "Lough" as in the first syllable of Lough-
borough.

Rindoon is an isolated place and even today is some distance from
the road. Knockskehan Hill rises to 329 feet but it means that any
landward approach must be made along a narrow slot of land in full
view of the defenders. But the importance of the fortifications
dates from the days when the lake was the main artery and Rindoon
commands the only navigable channel north and south. Isaac Weld
visited the remains in the summer of 1820, collecting material for
his Statistical Survey of the County of Roscommon:

> The view of the castle is extremely pleasing from the water,
> and more particularly so when the sheltered harbour beneath its
> walls receives a little fleet of the beautiful sailing pleasure boats,
> which are used upon this lake, the gaiety of whose ensigns and
> painted sides forms a remarkable contrast to the sombre tints of
> the ancient ivied walls.

It was not the castle or the view which commanded our attention
as we made our way ashore. Clad in plimsolls and light trousers we
found progress through the wild thickets of hawthorn and rose which
have engulfed the ruins, making them as inaccessible as any boiling
tar poured from the battlements would have done, a painful experience. Having got to that point where to retreat would have been as
difficult as to continue we found the arched gate of the keep. But
our route into the remains was barred by a deep moat which,
although not filled with water, looked just the place to engulf us to
our armpits in thick mud. We quickly understood why one of the
de Berminghams, members of the Anglo-Norman force which controlled Connacht, was heavily fined by his king for allowing this
place to be overcome by the O'Connors.

The Normans established their first castle here in 1227 when
Richard de Burgo was granted the lands of Connacht. The native

O'Connors were not pleased to see their lands taken and harried the Norman fortresses. The Normans retaliated and strengthened their forts until Rindoon, for example, resembled a fortified township. The first line of defence was a stone wall, around twenty feet high and running for 564 feet across the entrance to the peninsula. Half a mile further on and before the castle lay a ditch, once again extending across the entire peninsula, filled with water from the lake. The ruin which stands today is a great testimony to the skill of the Norman builders, although modifications were made in the sixteenth and seventeenth centuries, rather than to any Government department, since this important historical castle is being destroyed bit by bit as the ivy and creeper eats away at the mortar.

It is a place redolent of the barbaric times in which it was first built. A great vaulted cavern lies beneath the keep and we wondered how many prisoners must have languished there. The line of the walls and towers can still be traced, although you would be as well to equip yourself with a suit of armour to aid your progress through the undergrowth. In one corner stand the remains of a cottage but our thoughts that whoever had lived here, some shepherd perhaps, must have been something of a hermit were dispelled when we discovered an account of a Lough Ree voyage made in the 1880s by Mary Banim. Miss Banim contributed articles to the *Weekly Freeman* and these were collected and published as *Here and There Through Ireland* in 1891. At the time of her voyage the cottage was inhabited.

By the narrow causeway we enter the deep gateway, noting the vast thickness of the walls on every side and the extensive range of buildings that must have surrounded the inner court where now nestles the comfortable cottage of the caretaker of the lands —a hale old man, as brisk at eighty-seven as most men are at sixty-seven. In his home live three generations, according to a universal custom in all the country around; and not one of the family seems to have any shadow cast on his or her heart by the great keep or donjon hard by; they look upon the hoary walls as shelter from the western storms, and useful in their way, just as

is the fireplace of the old castle, useful now as the wide, cheerful
fireplace of the cottage; and the bright-eyed little girl who undertook to be our guide around the ruins little thinks, as she warms
herself at the blaze on a winter's night, of the strange figures that
often sat before those tall stone posts that frame in the cottage
hearth.

We were to see many sad abuses of ancient monuments during our
journey but this incorporation of the fireplace into the fabric of the
cottage has a charm all of its own.

Walking along the line of the moat we arrived at the remains of
what appears to have been a church and then, tiring of the ceaseless
battle through the thicket, we set out across the slope of the slight
ridge which runs like a backbone along the peninsula. Our way
ahead was effectively barred by the Norman wall which still rises in
places to a height of six and eight feet. No doubt the rest has gone
to build local farmhouses and cottages, as did the Roman walls of
the North of England. This defence had a central gateway which we
found to be closed by a rough wall on one side and fencing on the
other. A good place to shelter sheep in winter, no doubt.

Long before the Normans set foot on Irish soil the Norse under
Turgesius sailed their fleet up the Shannon into Lough Ree. How
they brought their craft up the estuary and into Lough Derg remains
something of a mystery but I can only surmise that they built flash
locks — walls of mud and wood — behind their craft, which raised the
water level so that they could travel forward some distance before
repeating the procedure. Such a method was certainly used on the
Severn before the invention of the gated chamber lock. It would
seem unlikely that the Norse did not take advantage of Rindoon's
strategic position.

There is a fabulous legend to account for the downfall of Turgesius.
Malachy was King of Meath and he had a beautiful daughter. The
King was ordered to send her to satisfy this tyrant's desires and this
the King did. But he also sent fourteen beautiful maidens with his
daughter and when the party arrived in the Norsemen's chamber
the girls threw off their gowns and revealed themselves as fourteen
fine Irish warriors. In the rout that followed the Norse were defeated

and Turgesius was captured and drowned in Lough Owel near Mullingar.

By now it was approaching noon and if we were to return in time to keep our appointment with Michael, it was time to leave this ancient stronghold. As we moved towards the shoreline the silence, with only the low howl of the wind in the trees and the bleating of sheep to be heard above the breaking waters, made us quicken our step. Dark clouds were tumbling down from the north and the mood of the lake was changing from one of playful frenzy to a serious, more menacing note. There are some places on this earth where even in daylight the memories of a bloody past make the loiterer restless. Looking back we saw a man on the ridge. Some shepherd, no doubt alarmed by the din which his flock had set up as we passed. We strode purposefully towards Safe Harbour, keeping to the shore to avoid the briars. As we climbed on to the deck of *Fenniscourt* I looked back to the ridge. The man had gone.

The cold chill running down my back soon turned to warm sweat. It was a simple job to release the mooring rope since Val had slipped it through the buoy ring and back on board. The anchor was another matter. Anchors have a splendid way of dragging when you lay them and then refusing to budge when you wish to leave. This was no exception. For a few nasty moments I thought we might have wrapped our chain around that of the mooring buoy—and I needed a night in the lee of Rindoon like I needed a hole below the water-line—but slowly I felt the chain slacken as the anchor slewed across the bottom. Then the chain came taut as the anchor rose suspended. Leaving Val to continue hauling in this heavy apparatus, which sadly needed a power winch, I raced to the wheelhouse and brought us out of the cove before the wind swept us ashore. Of course Val should have raced to the wheelhouse leaving me to haul in the anchor, but when you are standing on the bows of a drifting cruiser with a rapidly approaching gale you do not wait to debate the best procedure.

I was beginning to think that we had used up one of Vinny Farrel's spare lives as we took stock of our grazed legs and raw hands on the journey back to Barley Harbour. It had been a tiring morning's exploration but as we crossed the lake we felt a little like those early navigators as they returned from distant lands, exhausted but unbowed. We wondered how many people visited Rindoon. Not many, to judge by the undergrowth. There will be little point in anyone visiting the place at all if someone does not act to stem the tide of decay. If they do take the ruin in hand I doubt that the ghosts will flit – they have too secure a presence there.

Coming into Barley Harbour we were brought back into the twentieth century with a bang as *Fenniscourt Star* shuddered to a halt. It wasn't a rock we had hit but a tarpaulin which had been blown into the bay and was winding its way round our prop. Thankfully, after racing the engine into reverse and then holding it in neutral, we were able to clear this nasty obstacle. Michael came on board after lunch and we discussed the possible danger in leaving what little shelter the harbour provided. But the direction of the wind persuaded me that we would have to leave this place sooner or later and so, with Michael waving frantically to his wife as though he was bound for some transatlantic crossing, we headed *Fenniscourt* out into the wild waters of the lake. The following wind which had helped our passage that morning took us once more across Lough Ree, but instead of passing south we headed north-west through the safe channel between Iskeraulin and Wood Shoals and then turned into Blackbrink Bay. The anchorage Michael had chosen on the west side of the bay lay in a direct line with the narrow entrance and was too choppy for comfort. We moved across into a sheltered corner and made fast, with the usual gymnastics, to another mooring buoy. This was some distance from the point at which we wished to make landfall but with the outboard on the dinghy there was little need to exert ourselves.

Once on shore Michael led us up through the usual shelter belt of trees, the sheep and early lambs scattering before us, until we arrived at a tiny stone cottage swamped in flowering creeper. Here we were welcomed by Jimmy Furey. Jimmy is another worker in wood. He is part of a tradition which dates back as long as the people of the lakes can remember, for he builds the lake rowing boats, once the basic form of water transport and used by fishermen. The need for these sturdy craft has diminished since the building of the huge dam at Ardnacrusha and strict control of fishing by the Elec-

tricity Supply Board. But there are still enough customers to keep
Jimmy at his bench the year round.

Introductions over, we were ushered into Jimmy's workshop, a
stone shed tacked on to the gable of the house and tied so that the
interior was cool throughout the summer. In winter Jimmy has to
freeze as the abundance of wood chips is too great a fire hazard to
permit any form of heating. Here, amid the sweet-smelling mounds
of wood shavings, on which Jimmy's dogs, Jess and Brownie,
slumbered fitfully, we waded round the stocks on which lay the
beginnings of a Shannon sailer. She was being built for John
Fletcher, Honorary Secretary of the Lough Ree Yacht Club, who
has taken the helm of Jimmy's own SOD, No 108, for the last three
years. Jimmy and John have won the Long Distance race together
for the last two years. "With luck," said John, "and fifty per cent
of the Long Distance is luck, we'll make it a hat trick. And there's
no reason why the new boat, No 123, should not be a winner,
although Jimmy once let it slip that when he was building lake
rowing boats back in the thirties he knew how to make two apparently identical boats, one of which would win all before it and the
other would never know what it was to win."

These slim and elegant yachts, a development of the lake rowing
boats, first appeared at the turn of the century in events organised
by the local militia and gentry who were members of the Shannon
clubs. The Lough Ree Yacht Club is the second oldest in the world.
The earliest account of Lough Ree sailing has been preserved, along
with a great deal of other information that would otherwise have
been lost, by Athlone's local historian, Billy English. It dates from
1731. "A buck hunt was announced for every evening of the week,
a Regatta, a ball and other diversions." By the middle of the nineteenth century the practice was well established.

In August of each year, for a considerable time past (noted one
observer), a regatta has been held on Lough Ree. Hither flock the
fashion and beauty of the district for miles around; and once
more a fleet enlivens the aspect of the usually deserted lake. Gay
vessels decorated with many hand-coloured streamers, accompanied by bands of music and laden with gentlest ladies and

gallant gentlemen, glide tranquilly over the scene of many a well-contested battle.

Those were the days when gentlemen were gentlemen, and gentlemen had crews to do the dirty work. The boats were sloops and cutters with the occasional steam yacht owned by some English colonel. They were pukka days and the Union Jack still flew from the peak of the Commodore's barge. Some idea of those jolly boating events can be gleaned from the rules and regulations of the Killinure Yacht Club drawn up in August 1831.

> The members are always to appear on board their boats in the blue uniform (on the days mentioned in the 1st resolution) viz., Blue jacket with appropriate Buttons, Waistcoat White Cashmere with the Club Button, Trousers Blue, White or Chequered, as the member may think proper to wear.

The club secretary also thought it proper to inform the members that wine was "not allowed at mess, but the best spirits to be provided by the Purser". He was quite firm on the subject of servants. "One servant only to be served at the mess from each boat and two from the tender boat, and those to be under the immediate orders of the Purser."

Events could not have been more properly arranged had Nelson's fleet been approaching up the Shannon. But by 1889 the *Westmeath Independent* was describing the appearance of open centreboard dinghies and it was not long before a number of "queer-shaped things" were scudding across the waves. The days of the gentleman's regatta were numbered.

In order to bring about a degree of consistency, Morgan Giles was invited to provide specifications for a One Design craft. When the plans arrived they were costed and found to be too expensive and so the clubs on Ree and Derg threw out the 112-pound centreboard and replaced it with a fifty-six-pound one. Out also went the copper ballast tanks. With 140 feet of sail and a hull weight of less than 400 pounds the Shannon sailer was more akin to a torpedo than a racing yacht. Speeds in excess of twelve knots were quite common on the plane and until the end of the Second World War there was nothing with a length of eighteen feet and a beam of four foot six inches which could catch a Shannon One Design, SOD for short.

The design changes prompted Morgan Giles to disown the craft. He had been asked to produce a sailing craft which could race and also be used for a safe family weekend. But many well-known yachtsmen have admired the performance of the SOD, not least the late Uffa Fox whose visit in 1952 is well remembered, since that veteran of the waves had the misfortune to have his trousers drop to half-mast while taking part in the National Firefly Championships.

Beside Jimmy's workshop lay two new boats, their hulls covered with sacking to protect them from the sun. Beside these lay the frames of Shannon rowing boats past—a veritable graveyard in which Jimmy's young nephew was busy ripping the planking from an ancient frame. We were assured that this veteran would live to see another day since there was no trace of rot in the ribs. The boy was on holiday from college but when I asked if he would be following in his uncle's footsteps there was a sad shake of the head. Unless some young men take up this craft the day of the rowing boat and, more important, the future of the SOD will be in jeopardy. It would be a sad day to see these trim sailers replaced by plastic imitations.

The SODs had their heyday in the twenties and thirties if one is to judge by contemporary accounts. In these decades a fleet of larger craft would set off down the lakes to the place where the regatta was to be held. One such event, in 1923, almost saw the end of a long line of Shannon buffs. This is an extract from the log of the *Truant*, dated Tuesday, 21st August, 1923, which appears in L. M. Goodbody's excellent *History of the Shannon One Design Class*.

By twelve thirty a.m. the *Rambler*'s crew—never at any time good sailors—had completely lost their heads with terror. They hailed the *Shankshai* and begged for God's sake to send Micky Donnellon aboard. A punt was let back on the end of a line and Mickey climbed down the stern of *Shankshai*. He was then hauled up alongside the *Rambler* and got aboard. In the sea then running this was a great feat and no praise is too great for it. Once aboard he took the helm and things were again going well when the *Rambler*'s engines began to knock and in a few moments they stopped altogether.

The situation now grew rapidly worse. The *Rambler* swung broadside on and began to blow down on the *Shankshai*. The latter boat also broached to and in a short time the two boats came together at the bows. The rolling of the two was terrific and serious damage was suffered by both before they could be got apart. The two boats were rolling scuppers under and at one moment it was thought that the *Shankshai* was going over alto-gether. Healy – the skipper of *Shankshai* – gave the order to jump for it and he and Meleady managed to scramble onto the *Rambler*. The two boats at once rolled apart and it was some moments before Caesar (N. W. Early) was able to get aboard. On the *Rambler* all was chaos. Her crew were in a hopeless state – be-fuddled by drink and terror and the engine-driver would not even try and get his motor going. The crew of the *Shankshai* now took charge and endeavoured to get out an anchor and thereby get her head to wind. The fairlead in the bows carried away however and the chain ran along the beam and once again she was brought to broadside on. There was no opportunity of making the fall of the anchor chain and the four men – Healy, Meleady, Early and Donnellan—were forced to remain on deck holding on all night. With the rolling, two barrels of oil on the *Rambler*'s deck went overboard taking all the rail on the port beam and quarter with them.

Not surprisingly the remainder of that first day of the Lough Derg regatta "was spent repairing damaged boats and constitutions". As for ourselves we were glad that we did not come across this drama-tic evidence of the full fury of that lake until many weeks later. Had we done so beforehand we might never have embarked on our voyage. Although the antics of these early Shannon sailors "be-fuddled with drink and terror" might seem less than seamanlike there were many of their number who were masters of their art. Jimmy told us of one man, Otway Waller from Banagher, who set out from the Shannon on the four and a half ton yacht *Imogen* to sail single-handed to the Canary Islands. It was Otway Waller who pioneered the twin-staysail method of self-steering on the waters of Derg.

Jimmy built his first SOD, No 107, in 1971, having been taught the rudiments of his art from Walter Levinge of Athlone, the man who had built the first Shannon One Design trial boat *Phyllis*, later to be numbered out of sequence as 43, in the spring of 1921. Today the boats are still constructed in Jimmy's shed by the old time-worn methods. The planking is silver spruce or wych elm, riveted by hand; the stern is iroko; the magnificently fashioned rudder is made from one piece of mahogany. And the glory of these boats is as much in their making as in their handling. After the oak for the ribs has been selected, it is slotted into an old iron drainpipe leaning against a wall. The pipe is filled with water and a fire kindled at the closed end on the ground. When the wood emerges half an hour later it is not only supple enough to bend to the contours of the boat but is also jet black, contrasting well with the lighter hull. A recent client who did not want black ribs led Jimmy a merry chase, as he searched for a suitable length of clean pipe in which to boil them.

Jimmy's enthusiasm for his boats is to be seen everywhere and we were not surprised when he appeared with a model of a Shannon sailer, twenty-seven inches long and with a beam of eight inches. It had taken two months to construct, twice as long as the real thing. She was fully rigged and Jimmy had fashioned the interior out of bog oak. The brass fittings, correct in every detail, were worked by hand. It wasn't long before Jimmy and Michael were discussing the possibility of making a bog oak mount for this treasure. Strange as it may seem, these two craftsmen, the one working in the dead wood of the bog and the other in the new wood of the forest, had never before visited each other's workshop. Val suggested that the meeting was somewhat akin to that of Livingstone and Stanley.

Jimmy escorted us to the shore and we set off through the reed-shrouded margins to the outer lake. Looking back we could see our host stooped against the rising gale, his dogs at his heels, making his way back to the lonely cottage, to which the easiest access is by

5

water since there is no road entrance. Once out in the open water the demon of the deep took over, which is to say that the outboard ran out of petrol and spluttered to a stop. After refilling from the spare petrol can we discovered that no amount of pulling the starter cord would kick the engine into life and Michael and I set about rowing to *Fenniscourt*. With the wind against us it was like trying to row an ash tray. It was a back-breaking half hour and a wet one for Val who, sitting in the stern, received the full effect of every crab we caught. Once back on board, a full pot of tea was called for before any semblance of normal activity could be resumed.

Heading out into the main lake we discovered why our row across Blackbrink had been so arduous. The wind had risen and was howling around the canopy as the box waves, a phenomenon of inland seas, marched hither and thither in all directions. Thanking God and Guinness for a 72 HP engine we headed into this helter-skelter of water. As we entered Barley Harbour I realised that if we brought our craft any nearer than a few feet from the quay, we would be pinioned there until the storm abated which could take hours or days. We said our goodbyes to Michael on board and our pilot jumped manfully for the shore. With the engine racing we headed back into the lake, taking a southerly course for Athlone and the shelter of the narrow river section which leads to Lough Derg.

As we passed from the relative shelter of the Black Islands the shelf full of books in the saloon cascaded from port to starboard and the kettle, full of water, tried to jump across the companionway from the cooker to the sink. It missed and produced an instant river running up and down the cabin. Michael had suggested that we might visit the family who still live on the fastness of the Black Islands but no anchor would hold in such seas. Keeping our eyes peeled for the markers which would direct us safely past Adelaide Rock and Slate Rock we ran for the protection of Big Yellow and sudden tranquillity.

We were pleased to have reached safe water but were saddened at having missed a visit to the Black Islands. Michael had whetted our appetite with news of a recent escapade. A girl on the island took ill one winter and required drugs. The lake was frozen and Michael and some companions set off across the ice pushing a boat before them in case they should come to a thin patch. In retrospect, said Michael, it was a foolish enterprise since had the ice cracked and they had managed to get into the dinghy they would have been marooned with no way of making their way to the shore. The tale had a parallel in history since local people still talk of a funeral which set out across the ice from the islands. The ice gave way and many of the mourners were drowned.

FIVE

Shannon Other Designs

OUR ARRIVAL AT THE TOWN quay at Athlone was observed by a horde of small boys who were soon scampering around the deck clutching bags of worms which they wanted me to purchase. Being no fisherman I was unable to increase their pop quota, and in retaliation for my lack of interest a pair of them rowed off in the dinghy. It was some time before they returned, quite unabashed. As a result of this encounter we moved to a wooden jetty which lay behind a factory wall, hidden from the gaze of Athlone's worm-vendors. It was all that Val and I could do to drop into our bunks and sleep off the effects of a long day and a hard passage down Lough Ree.

The Shannon acts as a boundary between counties and provinces for much of its course and in Athlone the river separates the new town on the east and Leinster shore, from the old town on the west bank which lies in Connacht. As a result of this border position the town has been a heavily contested stronghold and it is possible that the bridge at Athlone has been destroyed and rebuilt more times than any other river crossing. In the tenth century the ships of Brian Boru swept up the Shannon by Athlone. In the twelfth century the O'Connor Kings of Connacht established a fort here and then the Normans built the first stone fortification. The tower of this early thirteenth-century castle still stands but the outworks have been wrecked or modified. The visitor no longer finds the castle towering above the crossing. That distinction is given to the Grand Canal Company stores beneath which a public lavatory provides ideal cover for any modern invader. Athlone was heavily fortified until the nineteenth century, thanks to the fear of a French invasion.

Upstream from the castle are Costume Barracks and the tourist guides will tell you how, in 1691, the brave efforts of a Jacobite soldier staved off the Williamite attack on the town. The garrison at Athlone numbered 1,500. Their attackers, under William's fellow Dutchman Jodert de Ginkell, numbered 18,000. The defenders were beaten back from the English town on the Leinster shore to the Irish fortifications in Connacht, but they destroyed part of the bridge as they went. William's forces managed a temporary repair but a skirmishing party, led by a sergeant of dragoons called Costume or Cushen, ran into the faces of the enemy cannon and put their torches to the repair. "Are there ten men here who will die with me for Ireland?" roared Costume, according to one account of the time. "A hundred eager voices shouted 'Aye.' Then we will save Athlone; the bridge must go down." And with it went Costume and his gallant volunteers. It kept back the attack for some time but eventually the defenders, well outnumbered, were put to the rout.

But a more detailed account of the battle, although it does nothing to belittle the actions of Costume, calls into question the whole strategy of King James's commander, Charles Chalmont, Marquis de St. Ruth. Throughout the siege St. Ruth's forces, which equalled Ginkell's in number, camped two miles from the town. Relays of soldiers were sent to assist the garrison but St. Ruth refused to install a larger permanent force. Meanwhile Athlone suffered the heaviest bombardment of any Irish city.

George Story, whose history of the campaign rings true when compared to those of other chroniclers, although he was chaplain to an English regiment and his brother was killed by the Rapparees, talks of Ginkell going through 12,000 cannon balls and six hundred bombs in the assault. St. Ruth's position at least made it impossible for Ginkell to send any large force across the river at a point to the north or south and so attack the Irish on their flank. What the French general might have achieved by carrying out such a manoeuvre himself and therefore trapping Ginkell against the Shannon we will never know. On the evening of 30th June around 2,000 English soldiers forded the river just below the bridge and found the breached walls in the hands of one of the regimental relays. These just happened to be the most inexperienced troops in the Irish army. The defenders could not retreat and neither could St. Ruth come to their aid since the rear and flank walls of the citadel still stood. "Never was town which was so well defended so basely lost," wrote one source, and the official newspaper, the *Dublin Intelligence*, reported: "One could not set down his foot at the end of the bridge, or castle, but on dead bodies."

The morale of those troops who went on with St. Ruth to meet the Williamites on a hill by Aughrim Castle near Ballinasloe must have been poor indeed. Once again St. Ruth had the advantage, with a hill defence protected by bog. But now the spot is commemorated by names like Gallows Hill and Bloody Hollow. St. Ruth attempted to instill a new vigour into his men. "King James will love you," he addressed them. "Louis the Great will protect you; good Catholics will applaud you; I myself will command you; the Church will pray for you; your posterity will bless you; God will make you all saints and His Holy Mother will lay you in her bosom." The final part of his speech certainly came true, at least for those who had taken Mass on that fateful morning. It was a Sunday. And Ireland fell.

St. Ruth was killed and to this day no one knows where his body lies. Henry Luttrell's cavalry were the first to retreat. He later received a pension from William. Their flanks unprotected, the Irish foot were butchered where they stood and only nightfall saved the remnants as the cries of the dying shattered the stillness of the bog. Seven thousand were killed and so died the flower of the army and nation and only the poets were left to record the lament. Yet the English noted great valour by their foes, with Irish troops leaping over the cheval-de-frise, the horrific spiked entrenchment designed to impale cavalry. Even Story's sober report notes that the Irish "behaved themselves beyond all expectations".

The Bridge of Athlone is a popular Irish tune but that last great battle of the Gael is most poignantly commemorated by the Chieftains, Ireland's accomplished band of minstrels, whose work is an example of folk art transcending the public image of that tradition. There are few more eloquent sounds than those created by the

Uillean pipes, manufactured with Irish cunning and a fair smack of irony, after the banning of the war pipes. When Paddy Moloney of the Chieftains puts his fingers to the chanter it is the sound of the poet you hear. The Irish pipes and the bodhran drums of Peader Mercier are used to full effect in Moloney's interpretation of the Battle of Aughrim. Here is the march to the battlefield, the strident holocaust itself with the bones marking strike upon strike, and then the lament and the tearful retreat.

I remember attending a Chieftains' concert on St. Patrick's Day in London's Albert Hall. The place was packed and from the gallery you would have needed *Fenniscourt*'s binoculars to have picked out the players on the apron stage. The playing of the battle was the great set piece of the evening. And there were other merrier tunes with Derek Bell's harp producing perfect counterpoint to the more expected flutes and fiddles. Bell's rendition of the blind Irish harper Carolan's compositions served well to remind us of the place of the harp in Irish music. Bell's much-waved white handkerchief — he's a lad from the north — reminded us of something else.

The Chieftains have been together for many years and it is this which has allowed Moloney to select and arrange the airs and jigs and Kerry slides which bring out the individuality of the group while retaining a sense of cohesion. They may play against each other and improvise with disgusting bravura, but as I wrote in a review at the time, it is the music that wins the battle.

Here, then, in Athlone, we have the place where the invaders of many centuries attempted to push the native defenders into the wild, barren lands of the west. "Out of the world and into Bodmin" was the way in which the English referred to that other Celtic stronghold of Cornwall. For Cromwell it was simply "To Hell or Connacht". Val and I walked past the unfortunately sited public loo and into hell, and a very fine inferno it was. They call it Sean's Bar. Here, in the old High Street, where the houses and shops cling somewhere between dereliction and demolition, is the rousing home of the first branch of the Inland Waterways Association of Ireland, founded on 19th February 1954.

The Williamite devastation of Athlone was not the last great battle of the bridge. That took place more than two hundred and fifty years later when a public inquiry was held in Athlone court-house into the fixing and lowering of Athlone road bridge. In 1952 there were no great hire fleets and therefore little commercial pressure to retain the original headroom. A year earlier the late Professor V. T. H. Delany had mooted the idea of a waterways association. Billy English, a local historian and keen waterman, wrote to the *Westmeath Independent* on the subject of the bridge. On 7th January, 1954, the first meeting of the IWAI was held in Dublin. Colonel Harry Rice—whose Shannon adventures have been preserved in the captivatingly titled "Thanks for the memory" —was President. Dr. Delany—author, with his wife Ruth, of The Canals of the South of Ireland—was Honorary Secretary, along with L. M. Goodbody—Historian of the Shannon One Design Class. They fought the battle of the bridge and won.

Boating had been positively discouraged until the creation of the waterways association which, according to Mr. Goodbody, had its genesis in the lavatory of a much-venerated Shannon boat, *Phoenix*, which we were to see later at Portumna. In the early fifties Mr. Goodbody moored *Phoenix* at Dromineer only to be met with a complaint from a local who drew his water from the lake. The North Tipperary County Council tried to pass a byelaw forbidding any craft from mooring within sixty yards of the shoreline which would have put much of Lough Derg out of bounds. If other councils had followed this example the Shannon today would be a watery empti-ness. As a result of this encounter which, luckily, did not pass into law, a group of Shannonites decided to form the association and this was later ratified at a public meeting in Dublin's Shelbourne Hotel.

The Athlone branch of the IWAI is still among the most active and apart from organising the annual week-long Shannon Boat Rally in conjunction with the Carrick on Shannon branch—the aptly sub-titled Shannonigans take place at the end of July—they have recently republished Colonel Rice's book. I had been in corre-spondence with Sean Fitzsimons, publican, waterway wizard and skipper of the most obscene-looking barge on the Shannon, *De Iron Lung*. Sean was in Dublin on our arrival in Athlone but we were bid a hearty welcome by his wife Anna, and it was not long before we were deep in conversation with everyone in general about nothing in particular. News of our imminent arrival in town had preceded us down the river, thanks to an efficient and mysterious waterway telegraph.

Sean's was in sparkling form that evening with Declan Walsh and Damion Byrne drawing excellent pints and a fiddler fiddling for all he was worth. All good things must come to an end and what a terrible end it is when all you can see in the bottom of your glass are the remains of that glorious creamy head and nothing but the promise of a sore one on the morrow. Anna has a most effective method of clearing the house at closing time. The temperature frequently hits the nineties, such is the heat of the conversation, but by opening both the back and front doors she manages to create a miniature hurricane which sweeps away the most recalcitrant imbiber. During the process Anna adjourns to *De Lung* for a cup of tea. On her return the place is empty and cleaning operations can begin. Our mooring at Athlone was peaceful, in spite of dire warnings from Sean's clan that our ropes might be cut in the night. This happened some years ago and the cruiser, thankfully unoccupied, was swept on to the weir below the town.

In the morning we went in search of supplies and discovered an excellent delicatessen which stocked all manner of luxuries, not least some fine continental cheese and meat. Cheese is expensive in Ireland with the rat-trap variety to be found in British supermarkets marked Irish Cheddar selling for twice the price in its country of origin. As a result of a hefty import tax Irish creameries now market a mock Camembert and Brie, and it would be doing soap manufacturers an injustice to compare these unpalatable spreads to their products. A real French farmhouse Brie decorated the deli's counter and breakfast took on something of a banquet spirit. It made a change from a previous meal we had in Athlone, when we noticed the magic word "salmon" on a restaurant menu and were surprised that a salad should only cost eighty pence. But here we were on a famous salmon river and perhaps the owner had been out the previous night. It certainly turned out to be cheap—cheap, tinned and Japanese.

As the cathedral clock announced eleven a.m. I decided that night had given way to day and that I should be disturbing no one on whom I might chance to call. Syd Shine's barge *Fox* lay just below the railway bridge and as I crossed the river in the dinghy I noticed that the entry hatch was cunningly placed on the water side. Syd has lived on the river since 1944 and I had been assured by friends in Dublin that no visit to the Shannon was complete without passing some time of the day on board his barge. *Fox* is something of a floating stately home with a pair of ornate iron gates leading on to the mooring at the Watergate. Once on board the image is in no way tarnished.

Fox was built by Grendons of Drogheda in 1865 and was used as a steam tug on the summit level of the Grand Canal before being converted to a maintenance boat. Dry-docked in the fifties she was declared fit only for scrap and snapped up by Syd for the princely sum of £50. Today she has been converted into a luxurious floating home complete with central heating and colour television. The ancient petrol/paraffin engine, which did its best to give Syd a hernia, has been replaced by a mighty 110 HP affair. But Syd is loth to do much cruising since every time he leaves his base the television must be roped to the floor and all the china cups and pots, which he has won, stowed safely away. His most treasured memento is a silver plate commemorating his service to the Lough Ree Yacht Club between 1965 and 1973.

Apart from the television set Syd is no man for modernity. He retired some years ago after quite a career as a musician and his band, Syd Shine and the Saints, made many tours round the halls of Britain. Back in Ireland he got down to the serious business of sailing his Shannon One Design, No 32, which he bought in 1956. There cannot be many dinghies more than half a century old which are still tacking and luffing but Syd's boat was the second SOD to be built, by Patrick Keneavy in 1922. "In 1969 or 1970," said Syd, "thirty-two had got into very bad repair and so I laid her up for two years and in the meantime ordered number ninety-two from Walter Levinge. I sailed ninety-two for two seasons with varied results, finding her good in light weather, but never very successful in heavy weather. I found that I was not really happy with her and decided to have thirty-two repaired and refitted by Peter Quigley. I've been sailing her ever since and I'm glad to say she's going strong and still winning the odd race and always well up in the fleet."

Syd had a sequel to the story about Morgan Giles. When man-made fibres began to replace cotton in the late fifties the Shannon clubs decided to make the change. The first set was hoisted on Syd's boat. Not only did she outrace everything in the water but she was in peril of splitting apart since the new sails held a great deal more wind than the old. Forgetting their earlier hurt the club sent the sails to Morgan Giles for his comments. He replied to the effect that this was what happened when a bunch of amateurs started tinkering with a perfectly sound design. First, chided Giles, you change the specifications of the hull and now you have the audacity to alter the sails. After all those years Mr. Giles was having his day of judgment. He did however indicate a modified sail area and the boats remain in one piece today.

Upstream from the *Fox* lay a sorry sight of a boat and I was astonished to find that this rusty lady was none other than *Tigh-na-Mara*, a photograph of which we had seen in L. T. C. Rolt's *Green and Silver*. It was hard to imagine that this was the same "veritable luxury liner" which came alive and glided smoothly across the water in 1948. Time had been cruel to *Tigh-na-Mara*, but try as I may I could not find two people who would agree on her pedigree or give two identical accounts of her fate. On a previous Shannon trip we had passed into the Inner Lakes of Lough Ree where Eyre Chatterton has a splendid wooded estate at Portaneena with safe moorings and much-used slipways. The weather had forced us to miss making this delightful detour again, but when I heard that Eyre was the nephew of a previous owner of *Tigh-na-Mara*, the late Bertie Waller, I contacted him in the hope of securing some accurate information. Eyre's reply was a masterly bit of précis writing, not lacking in wit. I have taken the liberty of quoting it in full since no amount of paraphrasing would improve his story. The letter is first dated 22nd June.

I always understood that *Tigh-na-Mara* was built in the United Kingdom about 1917 or 1918 and was put on the deck of a passenger ship. When torpedoed the passengers got into the lifeboat and shut all the deck hatches. As the ship went down *Tigh-na-Mara* floated off. She was converted into a motor yacht in the UK and fitted with two engines. When my uncle and aunt bought her in 1928 they sailed her over to Sneem in the Kenmare River (County Kerry) in the autumn; a very rough voyage. I stayed on her at Sneem in September 1929. My uncle then took her to Belle Isle (on the Shannon, near Portumna). My wife and I again stayed on her in 1935 and on Lough Ree in 1938 for the dapping (May fly). His name was A. G. "Bertie" Waller and he was in the Royal Flying Corps from 1915 to 1918 in France. His father (drowned with an Aunt near Meelick in 1892) converted the old weir mill at Banagher into a maltings.

Continuing Sat. 26th: How she ran aground is not clear; various stories. Most likely cause is that some malefactor cut her ropes in Terryglass Harbour where it is understood she was tied alongside the jetty. Then, in an east wind, she drifted unmanned with her drop keel down, and went aground on the west shore near Portumna. She was bought by the Athlone Sub-Aqua Club who salvaged her. They docked her at Shannon Harbour, welded on steel plates, and painted her bottom before bringing her to Athlone.

Not satisfied with his own account Eyre then contacted Bertie's widow, Mrs. Marjorie Chatterton, and in spite of failing eyesight she was quick to add her memories. Her letters came to me via Eyre with a typed transcription and it would only be correct to pay tribute to this fine old lady of the lake's efforts on my behalf. Mrs. Waller confirmed most of her nephew's story, adding that they had purchased the craft on the Thames at Chiswick and that she had spent part of the war on the deck of an Admiralty oil ship which was torpedoed. Whether or not *Tigh-na-Mara* fulfilled her original purpose and saved the crew is not known.

Eyre is developing his lakeside moorings and a new jetty is being built near an older harbour. Portaneena, originally Port an Shiona, the landing place of the wine, has long been associated with Shannon sailing having been the headquarters of the Killinure Yacht Club. In the nineteenth century a regular feature of any launching would

be the creation of a few lines of verse to commemorate the event and
Billy English has resuscitated one of these for his memoir on the
Lough Ree Yacht Club. It was composed by a Mr. Quinn on the
launching of Commodore Temple of Waterstown's yacht *Louisa*
on 21st May, 1833. Why the proceedings should have been dry is
beyond my comprehension. The report of the lassies dancing round
the bonfires makes me doubt the accuracy of the poet's quill, but
perhaps he had been reading too much Burns.

> The morning shone auspicious of this day,
>   And all repaired to Wineport's shore to see
> The launch so long expected at the bay
>   Of St. Helena Isle – the K.Y.C.

> Came on at intervals to grace the scene
>   Upon the beach where numbers did await
> The hour of two o'clock, the time between
>   Was filled with hopes and fears until that date.

> When grand the yacht in safety out did glide
>   Upon the ruffled surface of old Shannon
> Announced by cheers from side to other side,
>   And then confirmed by the discharge of cannon.

> For Admiral Digby gave a grand salute
>   From Wineport's heights, scarce equalled at the Nore,
> In days of Nelson's glory and repute
>   For famed *Louisa* and her Commodore.

> With thoughts delighted, home I bent my way
>   To Glasson village, thinking all was past
> When music softly, at McCue's did play,
>   The lighted bonfire appeared at last.

> Such merriment as now appeared to view,
>   Such sounds of minstrelsy as met the ear:
> What force of recollection can renew,
>   The scenes I happily did see and hear.

The bonfire burned and round a hollow square
 On circle of fire deep, I deem, was formed
Impervious to the view the dancing pair,
 Impregnable the circle to be stormed.

The dancing pair — oh, did I say the pair?
 If six I said 'twas nearer to the truth,
Small space to frisk was left the maidens fair,
 I went into McCue's, indeed, in sooth.

There hope presaged a little rest to find
 Perhaps a drink some neighbours would supply,
But disappointment met my anxious mind,
 All were intent on business, all were dry.

Thus having seen the whole I went to bed,
 And now I give the whole as I have seen,
Long live the Commodore to grace the shade
 Of Waterstown's long-known demesne.

We never found any poems about Eyre's Uncle Bertie but from
all accounts his exploits should have provided much inspiration for
some lakeside muse. In 1953, at the time of the first Long Distance
SOD Race from Dromineer Bay to Athlone, Bertie was running
astern of the dinghies. Once through Portumna Bridge he moored
for the night but, seeing a crowd of gongoozlers on the bridge, he
cast off, performed a couple of pirouettes in mid-stream and then
took *Tigh-na-Mara* under full power and wedged her bows firmly
on the island in the centre of the stream. He then summoned the
good folks on the bridge to close their mouths and put their backs
to the poles. *Tigh-na-Mara* must have weighed a good many tons
and it was some time before the hapless onlookers, encouraged by
her master in the wheelhouse, floated her off.

There are as many tales about Bertie's exploits as there are myths
and legends about Brian Boru. Among the many "queer-shaped
things" which punted about the river before the SOD appeared
there was, inevitably, a Waller invention. According to Mr. Good-

body this was *The Blazing Star*. She consisted of canvas stretched over plywood ribs, something in the manner of Aran currachs. "It was rumoured that she was made from hundreds of eel skins stitched together and that when hard on the wind her bows would turn round and look at you."

The best example of this Shannonite's sense of humour must be the Shannonigans which took place one day at Meelick lock. Mr. Goodbody tells the tale.

The reference to house-boats is of great interest for in those days, and for a number of years after the 1920s, the only method of travelling centreboards from one regatta to another was by water. A big fleet of house-boats visited all the regattas and the racing crews lived aboard or in tents ashore. There are several good stories told of the adventures of this fleet and probably one of the best concerns Bertie Waller.

Towing a long string of yachts behind his house-boat *Tigh-na-Mara* he entered a certain lock on the Shannon where he had on previous occasions crossed swords with the lock-keeper. According to the bye-laws he was only permitted to have one dinghy astern free of toll, and all the others were liable. He went ashore and paid for the *Tigh-na-Mara* and when told that he would have to pay singly for each of his tow, refused to do so on the grounds that the same lot of water in the lock would suffice for all, and having paid for it once for the *Tigh-na-Mara* he was not going to do so again. The lock-keeper, in duty bound, insisted, and Bertie had the whole string taken out of the lock and the house-boat locked through. He then proceeded to have his tow brought in one by one and paid for each singly. It was a hot day and after two had been locked through individually, the lock-keeper sued for peace.

Until 1844 a canal bypassed the river at Athlone, but our passage lay now southwards by way of the "new" Shannon Commission lock. The winding gear, with its mammoth two-man windlasses, is still stamped with Victoria's crown and the name of the manufacturer, Bankier and MacKenzie of Glasgow. One of the bottom gates dates from 1844 but this is shortly to be replaced. As we passed the mouth of the derelict canal the air filled with a vile stench. Pollution is not a major Shannon problem and surveys have shown that the water area is so large and the population so small that there is no danger to human life. But mightier rivers than the Shannon have been destroyed in Europe and Mr. Cooney, the Irish Minister for Justice, announcing a massive tourism and recreational study of the area, has already drawn attention to Athlone's unhappy habit of pumping raw sewage into the river. It seems odd that quite small towns and villages along the Shannon can install filter beds while Athlone cannot. Until Athlone does make some attempt to improve the situation the pong of the place ranks second only to the Scarriff Breeze, a nasty wind which whips across the lower part of Lough Derg, as the greatest hazard of the waterway.

SIX

Saints and Sinners

BELOW ATHLONE we ran between low callows or water meadows,
winter flood land. This broad, shallow valley continues almost to
Lough Derg, broken only by scattered hillocks of glacial drift and
dismembered esker ridges such as those at Shannon Bridge and
Banagher, the only crossing point in thirty-six miles although a foot
crossing is possible at Meelick, south of Banagher, by way of weir
and lock-linked islands. The cattle which graze this rich summer
pasture are the only living things you are likely to see. Clusters of
derelict cottages mark the old townlands, now uninhabited because
of the flood hazard. The area between Athlone and Shannon Bridge
has long suffered from inundation by the river. In winter the newspapers often carry astonishing photographs of new lakes far from
the river's normal course and a series of these photographs, published in 1965, showed the strategic importance of places like
Shannon Bridge, which lie on ridges above the floodline. While
water lapped their back garden walls the houses of the village stayed
dry and the road just passable.

There were no signs of the floods as we cruised south down river,
the course of which is split by a number of long islands. On reaching the second of these, Inchinalee, we had our first sight of
Clonmacnois with the sixty foot mass of O'Rourke's tower crowning
the horizon, as we followed the circuitous path of the river to the
landing stage.

Clonmacnois is one of the wonders of the Shannon, of all Ireland.
It is a place of saints and scholars, an ancient Mecca of Irish art

6

and literature, a truly holy city. And what is there now on the ridge of Art Tiprait, the height of the well, at Cluain-maccu-Nois, the meadow of the sons of Nos? The guide books list the masonry of the place: eight churches, two round towers, three High Crosses, four hundred early gravestones, two holy wells. Such documentation is their duty, but whatever they may say this place is still the Seven Churches of Clonmacnois. There are seven days in Creation, seven days in a week, seven graces, seven divisions of the Lord's Prayer, seven ages in the life of man and seven deadly sins. What guide book would, in the face of such evidence, contradict that there are seven churches at Clonmacnois, that Inis Clothrann is the Island of Seven Churches, and that Inis Cealtra on Lough Derg can be known as the Seven Churches of Asia round whose limits the pilgrims trod seven times?

But to stand on the great sloping hill which runs down to the slow swirling waters of the Shannon, as it meanders from Athlone to Portumna, is to feel the very eminence of the Gael at the beginning of our civilisation. It is a place where the eye may rove, the mind may dwell, and the intellect question. Here the introduction of Christianity stimulated and enriched Celtic culture. The riches were of sufficient merit, and the monasticism so firmly rooted, that the saints and scholars of Ireland might leave their native shore and settle in Britain, France, Italy and Germany. And students came from the Continent.

Our story begins on the Islands of Aran whose bouldered landscapes are thrown across the mouth of Galway Bay where it meets the long rollers of the Atlantic Ocean. Here is a place of mists and long winter nights of storm; where no tree grows and the howling oceanic wind hurls the salt water from shore to shore; where, in the summer, the islanders carry creels of seaweed from the beach to make thin layers of earth on their stone cropped fields. But Aran had its moment of shining light.

> Bright orb of Ara, Ara's sun
> Ah! softly run through Ara's sky,
> To rest beneath thy beam were sweeter
> Than lie where Paul and Peter lie.

One hundred and twenty-seven saints are buried in the church-yard at Killeany on Inishmore by the stump of a round tower and a shattered cross. Here are the islands of Synge's *Riders to the Sea*. Here is Aran of the Saints. It was to St. Enda's fastness that they came; St. Brendan the navigator, St. Columcille, who remembered Ara's sun as he was cast across the sea to Alba, and St. Ciaran, the architect and founder of the first wooden church at Clonmacnois. St. Ciaran arrived here, having travelled from Inis Ainghin on Lough Ree where he had set up another ecclesiastical centre, some time between A.D. 538 and A.D. 545. The silver moon of St. Ciaran stayed by the Shannon and "Ireland at her centre gleamed". Seven months later the founder died and he was buried in the first church, the entrance afterwards stopped with stone. There is a Biblical analogy between the life of Christ and that of this Irish saint who is said to have died at the age of thirty-three. His father was a carpenter.

We shall never know why the saint chose this site. Was it the loneliness of the setting where only the curlews' cry pierces the fumbling murmur of the reeds? Was it nightfall and the ridge of the esker which forces the Shannon to twist and turn on its course seemed to offer safety and promise of a dry encampment? Whatever the reason it was a bad place to choose. The islands of the loughs were tree girt and sheltered from storms. Their number was a form of protection from heathen invaders since it was something of a lottery to know which one they would single out for abuse as they passed. But here at Clonmacnois the ridgeway captures the vehemence of every wind which blows across the bog and river and it lay on the very route the Norse invaders were to take on their way inland from the sea.

The holy city was put to the torch no fewer than thirteen times between 722 and 1205, and was plundered by the Vikings on eight occasions. Turgesius gave it his usual attention in 844 and his wife Ota desecrated the altar by celebrating pagan rites. In spite of these attacks Clonmacnois continued to grow and the monks always returned to re-establish their place of worship on the departure of the invaders. This was no place of hermit monks but a thriving township which included craftsmen and a small armed guard,

although the latter would only have seemed able to cover the retreat of the citizens into the no man's land of the bog. In 1179, the
date of a Norman attack, we know that one hundred wooden houses
were destroyed. It was English troops who eventually brought ten
centuries of religious and scholastic glory to a close in 1552. No
doubt Clonmacnois was a pleasant afternoon's pillaging from their
fortress at Athlone. *The Annals of the Four Masters* tell that they
did their work well and that not "a bell, small or large, an image or
an altar or a book, or a gem, or even glass in a window" avoided
their attentions.

But some of the great manuscripts prepared at Clonmacnois
were saved; the twelfth-century *Leabhar na hUidhre*, the Book of
the Dun Cow, which contains one text of the *Tain* among other
heroic sagas, the earlier *Annals of Tighernach*, after the eleventh-
century abbot of the same name, and the *Annals of Clonmacnois*
itself. But the greatest memorials of this ancient place are the
buildings which still stand, their roofless outlines firmly set against
the sky beyond the ridge. To savour the silent pageant of Clonmacnois it is best to arrive by water as its founder did. Go early in
the morning or follow the setting sun when the place has shaken
off the bellowing tripper who finds the ancient stones best suited
for use as picnic tables. Then you will understand the glories celebrated in the medieval Irish poem, translated into English by the
nineteenth-century poet and scholar, T. W. Rolleston, in 1888:

In a quiet watered land, a land of roses
    Stands St. Ciaran's city fair,
And the warriors of Erin in their famous generations,
    Slumber there.

There beneath the dewy hillside sleep the noblest
    Of the clan of Conn,
Each below his stone, with name in branching Ogham,
    And the sacred knot thereon.

There they laid to rest the seven kings of Tara,
    There the sons of Cairbré sleep,

Battle-banners of the Gael that in Ciaran's Plain of Crosses,
  Now their final hosting keep.

And in Clonmacnois they laid the men of Teffia,
  And right many a lord of Breagh.
Deep the sod above Clan Creidé and Clan Conaill,
  Kind in hall and fierce in fray.

Many and many a son of Conn the Hundred-Fighter
  In the red earth lies at rest,
Many a blue eye of Clan Colman the turf covers,
  Many a swan-white breast.

It was the communion of the many clans at Clonmacnois, noted
in these verses, with no race claiming it as their own, which accounts
for the long survival of this university. As we see from the ruins
which still stand they were built by many hands – the O'Connors
of Connacht, the O'Kellys, the Mac Dermotts and the O'Rourkes
all built their churches and towers here. As we made our way up
the gentle slope to the trim lawns and paved walks which circle the
monuments the sky was leaden. If St. Ciaran had merely been
seeking an austere setting he had found one. A brisk wind tormented
the waters of the river and whipped round every corner and through
every window socket.

There is hardly a tourist manual which does not describe in detail
the dates and uses of the ruins at Clonmacnois and, having read a
good many of them, and some more scholarly works dealing with
excavations there, I find myself totally confused. Many of the early
stone churches were rebuilt or had extensions added at a later date
and some of these additions were constructed from stone cut at an
earlier date and plundered from another ruin. The result is not so
much a jigsaw puzzle which time and patience will solve, as an
architectural porridge which I would not like to stir further.

The effect of Clonmacnois does not rely on one or two particular
buildings but is total; the churches strewn haphazardly about the
slope, bearing testimony to the Irish habit of erecting many citadels
rather than one vast cathedral. St. Ciaran's Church is the most

revered spot. Barely twelve feet long the stonework is a hotch-potch of dates, although the earliest may be eighth century. It marks the place where the patron is supposed to have been buried. Surrounding it, on three sides, are later buildings. In the north-west corner of the rough square which marks the present-day boundary is O'Rourke's tower, more than sixty feet high. In 1135 the conical cap was struck by lightning. The monks of Clonmacnois must have been well acquainted with the inside of this place during the many raids on their city.

Amid all the buildings stand ancient stones and crosses, given some order by recent improvements by the Board of Works to whom the site was presented by the Church of Ireland in 1955. It is the sandstone crosses which provide the most eloquent memorials to the saints and kings who lie buried in this place. Before the door of the cathedral stands Cros na Screaptra, the Cross of the Scriptures, erected by Abbot Colman in memory of Flann Sinna, King of Tara, who died in A.D. 916. The foot of the shaft carries a worn inscription which has been deciphered as reading: "Pray for Colman who put this cross over King Flann. Pray for Turcan, who made this cross." No one seems to have bothered praying for King Flann. It is one of the most ornate ancient crosses I have ever seen, with more than fifty figures and a series of sculptured panels chiselled out of the sides of the shaft. These show the arrest of Jesus, the guard at the tomb, the Crucifixion and the Last Judgment.

One of the bottom panels shows a scene out of context with the others. It has been interpreted as showing a warrior and a monk holding a rod on top of which a bird is perched. The monk is said to be St. Ciaran and the soldier Diarmaid Mac Cerbhaill of the royal house of the ui Neill who helped St. Ciaran to lay the first foundation. Two other High Crosses, known as the North and South Cross, also carry an unusual amount of well-preserved carving.

Beyond the enclosure of the churches and the gravestones a narrow road leads to the Nun's Church. A certain amount of restoration work took place here in the mid-nineteenth century but it appears to have been done with care. The richly carved west doorway and magnificent chancel arch were re-erected then. The building stands in a field in a slight hollow and is surrounded by some of the few trees whose backs have not been broken by the gales. Here it was that Dervorgill erected her church as a penance for the treachery she committed and which brought the Norman invaders.

Here it was, if I may break the spell of this place, that it began to rain. As we scurried along the road back to the main settlement it was not that soft Irish rain of which the natives are forever telling, but a thick and thunderous downpour which set the clouds rumbling overhead. We ran into a church and, of course, it was roofless. We ran down to Temple Finian where a canopy has been erected over a modern altar, but the wind swept the rain through the open sides till it formed puddles at our feet. During a lull in the storm we made for the jetty at the double.

Time was when the ruins of Clonmacnois were left to the wind and the weeds. Today, thankfully, they have been saved from complete decay. But there are two intrusions. The modern canopy which covers the present place of open-air worship is a vulgar edifice with clattering tannoys projecting from the eaves. The other misfortune is a concrete walled avenue which leads into the grounds from the car park. The rare collection of fragmented gravestones and crosses which littered the site have actually been embedded in the mortar, a very insensitive way in which to treat such relics. Not only that, but the job has been badly done and some of the stones are already coming away from their setting.

For the remainder of the afternoon the rain continued to sweep across the river in wild grey curtains and it set up a magnificent tattoo on the cabin roof which would have been the joy of many an Irish drummer. Even the ducks seemed to have called it a day. Just as we were beginning to think that the winter floods had made a re-appearance the rain stopped abruptly. A mighty rainbow arched across the ruined monastery and the buildings glistened in the thin bright light which comes after the storm. It was a vision which no camera could hope to capture. After supper ony a few patchy white streamers hung in the sky and in the west we could see the promise of fair weather ahead. But Irish weather is fickle and so we took advantage of the calm to walk the Pilgrim's Road.

The Ordnance Survey map showed a pleasant circular route

which would lead past a scattering of houses and a school, the townland of Clonfinlough. A number of lanes and cart tracks spread-eagle themselves over this tiny elevated place and it was around here we knew that a stone far older than anything at Clonmacnois still lay. The network of tiny lanes was making our search difficult until we found a man pushing his bicycle downhill. Did he know where we might find the stone? He did, he said, adding that no one ever went near the place. His directions were simple. Follow the telegraph wires. The wires led us to a church and we knew that the scent was getting warm. We climbed a gate and walked along a newly-constructed path which stopped dead at a seemingly im-penetrable thicket of briars. Moving to our right we came out through stunted scrubland on to a tiny bare hill and a fabulous view of the bog with Fin Lough in the foreground and the sun casting a fiery crimson light across the brackish water. A great clatter of geese rose from the tiny lake but although there were plenty of boulders about, none fitted the description of the one we were looking for. Retracing our steps we peered through the thicket at the path's end and, sure enough, there was a stone. It was quite another matter beating our way through to the field in which it lay, but at least when we did so it was the right place.

Here, at Cluainn finn loch, the meadow of the white lake, lay the stone with that name. It is a large flat-topped boulder etched with many curious scribings. The most common of these is a vertical line with a blob at the top, the line piercing a rough oval. Another shape is similar but is in the form of a cross. R. A. S. Macalister, in con-sultation with a French archaeologist, was able to place this in the Neolithic period but what was more astounding was that similar shapes were found by his French colleague, in Spanish cave paint-ings. The circular figures are said to represent the victors, and the crosses, the dead. If this was some ancient battle site the place was well chosen.

There were more showers in the night as we lay in the shadow of the monastery but when we rose it was with the sun. We left St. Ciaran's city fair and travelled south by Devinish Island and Long Island to pass beneath the majestic sixteen-arch crossing at Shannon Bridge. The swing arch has been replaced by a Bailey bridge which makes a dreadful racket every time a vehicle passes over and we had been advised by our friends in Athlone to continue on for a few hundred yards to where an island creates a pleasantly sheltered creek. This island, which lies at the confluence of the Shannon and the River Suck, was unidentified on all our maps save Colonel Rice's chart where he gives it the name Borniagh.

Although a less important crossing than Athlone, the remains of Shannon Bridge's historical past have avoided the developer's ball and chain and you can spend a full day rambling the unique fortifications which stand on the west bank. But first the traveller may wish to quench his thirst in Killeen's hostelry where the sons of the house, Derry and Michael, extend a mighty welcome to travellers by water. The township consists of one main street lined with cottages, some trellised in a glorious riot of colour, shops and a completely disproportionate number of bars which open when the mood takes them, or when the owners' cows have been milked. By some quirk of fate Killeen's, the establishment most favoured by Shannon boatmen, is furthest from the river. Perhaps the walk back to your boat is designed to concentrate the mind, thus avoiding collapse into the Shannon.

It is another old Irish bar and lurking behind the modern bay window lies a snug, dark place where your pint is drawn as though all the saints up the road were taking note of the performance. You can step through into the shop next door where you can buy anything from a needle to a haystack. To call it a grocery would do it less than justice. Above the tinned soup is a box marked *pyjamas—men's*, next to it another announces *pants—woollen*. Of course most people make the passage from the clothing and food department into the refreshment section—it is a variation of the dog-walking syndrome. You can almost hear the men of Shannon Bridge telling their wives that they are just going down the road to Killeen's for some *pyjamas—men's*. Once ensconced you come under the sardonic grin of George Brent whose autographed photograph hangs askew above the fireplace. Mr. Brent was a little before my time but although I was assured that he was born in the village and shown the family house, no one could remember any of his films. I am indebted to the *Guardian*'s film critic, Derek Malcolm, for the information that George Brent was the celluloid name for a Mr. G. B. Nolan whose career began in the thirties. Among his films was *42nd Street* and *The Painted Veil*. In 1941 he starred with Bette Davis in *The Great Lie*. In all Shannon Bridge's most famous son made more than two hundred Hollywood films and, for some reason best known to himself, Derek was keen to point out that he wore a hairpiece.

That evening Derry introduced us to Patrick Joseph MacDermott, a local farmer who was to prove a fount of knowledge on the social history of the area, being a well established part of it himself. As he was accompanied by some friends that evening we arranged to meet the following afternoon. Such arrangements are often made and seldom kept, but the next day Pat Joe, as we had been commanded to call him, was trundling his bicycle down the road to the river. We strapped it on the bows and set off to moor below the Bord na Mona railway bridge which takes turf to the power station from the bogs on the west bank of the river. Pat Joe seemed so comfortably situated in the cockpit, with a smile on his face and a glass in his hand, that we passed the mooring and continued down river for a while as he pointed out his own secret places of note along the banks. The water was teeming with life, sandlarks and bald headed coots and cranes. But it was the life underwater which commanded the attention of Pat Joe. There was not a hole in the river which he did not seem to know for its trout and eel potential. We were careful to avoid the subject of salmon since it is considered bad manners to question any fishermen on this matter.

At one spot Pat Joe explained that this was where a one-legged friend had fallen from his boat during a shooting expedition. The gentleman was alone at the time and no one could understand how he had made it to the bank. Pat Joe could only presume that his wooden stump had kept him buoyant. When the good man reached the shore he marked the spot before rushing off in search of dry clothing. A few hours later he was back with a grappling iron to retrieve his best gun which had gone over with him. It is still worrying the wildfowl on the river to this day.

Before the bog railway bridge was built the people of Clonfert Callows, where Pat Joe lives, were cut off from their nearest sup-

plies in Shannon Bridge by the River Suck, which enters the
Shannon from the west bank north of the town land. As a result
most people had a rowing boat. The river is treacherous at the
confluence with the Suck and many hair-raising incidents took
place, particularly in winter. Pat Joe recalled one occasion when he
left Shannon Bridge in thick fog with a strong stream running. He
was congratulating himself on having made the passage downstream
but his pleasure on setting foot on dry land was marred by the
appearance of an enormous creature on the bank. Pat Joe had landed
at the wrong place and as the mist rolled away the huge bulk of a
neighbour's bull was to be seen preparing for the coup de grâce.
Nothing was going to get Pat Joe back in the water and so he set
out across the field with what was surely a reincarnation of
Turgesius at his heels. As he said, he's here to tell the tale but only
just.

The railway bridge is an unsightly concrete affair but it has been a
blessing to those who live on the "wrong" side of the Shannon.
Local car drivers think nothing of crossing it in the wildest of storms,
and when I had suggested the previous evening in Killeen's, that it
must be a dangerous route with no retaining wall to save the careless,
a lady leaned forward and assured me that she "just kept the
wheels locked to the outside of the tracks and prayed to St. Ciaran".

Coming to the bank below this bridge we walked along the track
and then down a narrow metalled road to Pat Joe's house where his
dog, Sarah, made her presence known by trying to snap at our
heels. Apparently introductions had not been properly made and
after a great deal of petting and ball-throwing she sloped off quite
merrily. Today Pat Joe lives in a tiny though modern asbestos and
concrete chalet which consists of two rooms leading off a central
living area. Sitting ourselves round a vast iron stove which took up
most of the wall, Pat Joe set about preparing tea on the turf fire
which he lit within seconds by the simple expedient of dousing it
generously with paraffin. Pat Joe thought the range a little large
for the room but, as he said, "when I visited the ironmonger it was
that or nothing so I had that. It's a number nine".

Men like Pat Joe MacDermott usually only exist in works of
fiction; men who may not be rich in the hardware of modern life but

who have a wealth of knowledge to impart and a way of telling their tales that makes you feel not an intruder but a participant in an ancient oral tradition. Here the art of conversation and storytelling was to be found at its richest, without any need for a drop of the hard stuff to oil the intellect.

Pat Joe is a small farmer with some thirty head of cattle which he fattens in the meadows around his home. The place is spartan but he would ask you what more a single man might want. He keeps a couple of milk cows and a few chickens for eggs and with these he barters for potatoes and the occasional bit of pork. He does not know when his family first arrived in the area but imagines they were probably forced to move to these bad lands – the floods which create the rich summer pasture only date from the building of the dam at Ardnacrusha – in Cromwell's time. The house and the lands are like an extension of his body. His chalet lies below the walls of the old stone-built family house and he showed us the ruin of the very room in which his cradle lay. Ripping decades of bracken and nests from the fireplace, he showed us the crane on which the pots were hung over the open fire. Behind the ruined house stand the cattle sheds and pig sheds, the latter having their own fireplace where the pig food was "biled". Down the road the family well still provides pure water, so thick in iron that the bucket has a thick yellow ring around the rim. According to Pat Joe a "man came down from Dublin and declared the water genuine", which was just as well since we were on to our second pot of tea.

"In the old days," Pat Joe told us, "the barges used to pass to and fro with their loads of stout and porter and one evening a barge hit the tip of Borniagh and the deck cargo got drowned in the river. We were fishing the stuff out for months afterwards and Guinness, accepting the inevitable, just put up a notice at the Post Office at Shannon Bridge asking if they could have their *empty* barrels back. One of my neighbours fetched one up a full three months after the accident but I didn't touch a drop until the lads from the bog were singing their hearts out. Then I went up with the kettle. For, you see, I didn't know what three months under water might have done to the stuff. I had to make sure it hadn't turned to poison. It was as sweet as a fine woman that has lost her head. And it had, too."

We had read how the barge crews would bore tiny holes in the barrels and extract a few pints from each during the journey, stopping the holes afterwards. Pat Joe had a sophistication to add to this event. Apparently some of the crews hammered up the barrel hoops so that when the new bung was inserted and the hoop replaced, no trace of their handiwork could be seen. Everywhere we went someone would tell us of this traditional pilfering and we wondered if the old Guinness casks were not more bung than barrel.

Another great game concerned the whiskey barrel which used to be delivered to the publican who would then decant the contents into bottles. These were too small and too well checked to be tampered with but when empty, the crews would pour a pint of boiling water into the barrel and add a pound or so of sugar. Shaken, not stirred, the water teased the whiskey which had been absorbed into the wood and a mighty punch was the result. Now we knew why we had never seen an old canal barge which didn't have a fair number of dents in her bow.

A great deal is told of the way in which the small farmers rely on the dole but Pat Joe was keen to inform us that he had never bothered with this "farmer's pension" as it is called. "In any case, it may only be a mile to Shannon Bridge but that is in Offaly. Here we are in Galway and my nearest registration town is Ballinasloe. And what man is going to cycle seven miles there and seven longer miles back to pick up a few pounds."

As dusk began to fall it was time to bid farewell to Pat Joe and we left him and Sarah to their lonely idyll and made our way down to the river. Once on board we discovered that while our mooring had been easy to enter it was not so easy to leave. The current swirling round the arches kept us pinned to the bank and there was a great deal of heaving and poling before we were far enough from the bank to make the turn through the navigation arch. We were keen to explore the ruins up-river since among the many books and papers the Killeens had showered on us was a paper on the fortress by Paul Kerrigan, an Athlone teacher.

The Shannon has always been a natural entry for invaders making their way to the geographical centre of the country. The Vikings arrived there in A.D. 835. The yoke which the Norse put round

Ireland was not broken until that most legendary of Shannon chiefs, Brian Boru, urged resistance. He succeeded in quelling the Norsemen, sometimes with the assistance of and sometimes in spite of Malachy, King of Meath. In 1002 Brian achieved supremacy when he met his rival at Tara. Malachy surrendered and Brian, the Shannon king, took the High Kingship and laid claim to the monarchy of the entire Celtic race. He set about establishing another great age of Irish culture, rebuilding churches and places of learning destroyed by the Viking hordes. In 1013 Viking aid from Orkney, Scotland and Man was given to the disruptive forces of the Dublin Leinster alliance and Brian Boru set out from the Shannon on his last battle. The Norse sagas speak of Brian's Battle but there was no winner of the rout which took place at Clontarf on Good Friday, April 23, 1014. Too old to do battle Brian remained behind the lines and there he was killed, slain by a retreating Norseman. So died the Shannon king, and with him a heroic age came to an end. Once again Ireland was to come under the control of weaker men whose internal squabbles led to minor provincial wars. The fortifications at Shannon Bridge are from much later wars.

When war broke out with France in 1793 new fortifications were constructed throughout Ireland and the Martello towers around Dublin date from 1804, a year earlier than those placed around the coasts of Kent and Sussex. Further work was undertaken along the line of the Shannon since Galway Bay and the Shannon estuary both ranked high as possible invasion points. The quickest route from Galway to Dublin is via Shannon Bridge, with Athlone calling for only a slightly longer haul. As a result both these points were well defended since it was thought unlikely that any invasion force pulling heavy artillery would leave the main highways, such as they were. As we walked into the *tête de pont* or bridgehead we were quickly made aware of its strategic importance. The main road to the bridge sweeps through the fortifications with callow swamp, impassable by heavily armoured troops, on all sides. One barbaric act was carried out by the local county council when they destroyed the arched gateway across the road. This was done so that the road might be widened. Since the bridge has remained single track, the traffic flow controlled by lights, the operation appears completely

pointless. Now there are even plans to bypass the town by building
another bridge.

The stone fortresses remain. The grandest feature is a bomb-proof
barracks on which were mounted four guns. Opposite is the redoubt,
its construction thought to be unique in Ireland. We entered by a
sunken road which would have given protection to the defenders.
The front face of the redoubt consists of a partly artificial slope of
some two hundred yards, so designed because this was the effective
range of a musket at the time. A dry moat separated the slope from
the main wall of the redoubt and into this ditch projected a
caponiere, with a vaulted stone-flagged bomb-proof roof topped with
slates. The floor of the passage lies below ground level to give the
guards a better line of fire. We plunged into this dungeon-like hole
with narrow slit windows and found that a farmer had erected crude
concrete walls to make a byre of the place. Enterprising this may be
but we wondered what the next act of vandalism might be.

Although these massive fortifications were never put to the use
for which they were designed, the landing of 1,000 Republican
soldiers under General Humbert in Killala Bay on 22nd August,
1798 made their construction appear a reasonable precaution. On
the east bank of the Shannon at the entrance to the village stands a
sturdy square stone house which carries a sign to the effect that this
was the office of the Shannon Commission official, no doubt the
bridge-keeper who would also have been in charge of the wharf.
In fact the wharf below the bridge is all that remains of a lock which
became redundant in the 1840s. The house would make a splendid
riverside home, were it not for the din set up by the Bailey bridge.
A few yards further up the main street a great stone arch, badly
decayed, is all that remains of a barracks built to house soldiers
during the building of the main defence. This was demolished by
the Office of Public Works and in its place has sprouted, appro-
priately enough, the local Gardai station.

Fenniscourt's estimated times of arrival had become something
of an Irish joke. We had spent the best part of two days in Shannon
Bridge and our next plan, to reach Portumna by nightfall, was to
be defeated by darkness. Passing down the river we came to the
island which marks the confluence with the River Brosna where a

large painted sign announces the entrance to the Grand Canal. It was hardly visible as we passed. The birds set up their last songs of the evening and although the moon lit the channel well enough for easy navigation, we decided to stop overnight at Banagher. We were soon gliding past the modern wooden jetties and just before passing under the bridge we turned off into the old Grand Canal Company Harbour. Although the river seems wide and deep here, we were careful to follow the marked course. Many of the markers are set on cairns on the edge of rocky underwater outcrops and we were not surprised to find that Banagher's Irish name, Beannchor, signified a place of pointed rocks.

Astern, the reflection of the arches of the bridge was held in the water like a colour negative. A donkey ambled across the bridge. As I switched off the engine the silence surrounded us with only the occasional plop of a fish in the water to be heard. There were signs of life behind the canal company shed where an enormous tinker camp fire spluttered and sparked. It was the same group that we had met on previous visits, which rather contradicts the title of itinerants which the Irish have given these people. One of their number, a visitor from Clonfert, had come over from Kent. He had been born on the road near Maidstone and spent the first twenty years of his life in the hop fields and orchards of the garden of England before coming to Ireland. When I asked why he had moved he said: "There's less hastle."

As the hour was late we decided not to disturb our friends Malcolm and Ingrid MacDonald who live in a house above the town. We would return this way to visit the Grand Canal. It was the MacDonalds, however, who had first put the thought of writing this volume into my head. When we had met the previous year, Malcolm had presented us with a rare copy of L. T. C. Rolt's *Green and Silver*, the story of another Shannon voyage. In 1946 this intrepid English engineer and inland waterways enthusiast had set off from Athlone in a converted ship's lifeboat and spent a number of exciting months on the Shannon, completing a circular route by way of the Grand and the now derelict Royal Canals. Rolt's *Narrow Boat*, first published in 1944 and telling the story of his

Her Victorian Majesty, *Phoenix*, 103-year-old gentleman's steam yacht, before restoration (above) and after (below)

The round tower and a ruined church on the holy island of Inis Cealtra at the mouth of Mountshannon Bay.

An eagle's view of Lough Derg from the Tipperary shore looking north-west. The point on the left is Aughinish where the cruiser ran aground, and beyond it the tower of Inis Cealtra is just visible.

conversion of the narrow boat *Cressy* and subsequent voyage around England on her, has become something of a Bible among Britain's canal buffs.

I bought a first edition of *Narrow Boat* many years ago, while planning our own similar voyage, and had marvelled at this famous navigator's journeyings at a time when canal pleasure craft were enough to cause the owners of traditional working boats to collapse in the cut in astonishment. I have seen a plan of the *Cressy*, an original Shropshire Union Canal fly boat converted to power with a Ford Model T engine, and the luxury encompassed by her seventy-foot hull would make many of today's factory-built boats appear like hulks. The part I particularly liked was the bathroom, the creation of which caused some problems for Mr. Rolt. The first short bath of his choice was too large to pass through the entrance doors and it took a great deal of searching before one of the correct size could be found. As the cabin floor lay below water level Mr. Rolt proceeded to mount his bath on a plinth so that the water could run out through the hull without the need of a pump. Today's canal craft, with their powerful diesel engines capable of charging banks of batteries, are usually fitted with a shower but we were pleased to see a new craft at our own moorings at Braunston, Northamptonshire, which might well have been inspired by the *Cressy*. *Fawndale*, as this new boat is called, had recently been delivered to the marina and naturally we were to be found peering through the windows. To our surprise we saw just the kind of sitting bath which Mr. Rolt must have used. We were not surprised to hear later that *Fawndale*'s owners were plumbers.

Over the years I had been building up a library of L. T. C. Rolt's works but had never obtained *Green and Silver*. In fact I had no idea what the book was about until Malcolm gave us a copy. We spent the remainder of our voyage that year referring to it and we were astonished to discover how little the Shannon had changed. In fact we came across lock-keepers, as at Tarmonbarry, who were still manning the same Shannon gates. It was this which prompted us to search out more closely just what had happened to this great river in the intervening years.

Of one thing we were sure. Nothing had happened to Banagher

7

since *Green and Silver* had been written. Mr. Rolt thought that the place had resigned itself to slow decay but unless, like all movement in Ireland, this proceeds at a slower pace than elsewhere, I can only suggest that the village has been touched with a palsy which has cast it into the land of Rip Van Winkle. The same dingy façades predominated and even the derelict properties looked as though they had been built that way. There is one bright spot in the main street where the proprietor of the hardware store has retained the traditional painted stonework, but instead of having his decoration confined to the corner stones, the lozenge effect stipples the entire street frontage. And a very fine old-fashioned hardware store it is, with knives and forks, strainers, pots and pans and other utensils hanging from the ceiling beams. Perhaps one day Banagher will waken from its slumbers but it certainly was not considering any movement on the Saturday night of our arrival. That splendid Irish wit Hugh Leonard, writing in *Hibernia*, described the liveliest thing there as a dead cat. That was on a Good Friday, but even on less holy days it takes a great deal to stir Banagher.

The town has its claim to a place on the tourist map of Ireland, although I find its reason for being there more astounding than profound. How did Anthony Trollope ever find the inspiration to write two novels, *The Mac Dermot of Ballycloran* and *The Kellys and the O'Kellys* in this place? Perhaps there was little else to do during his stint as Post Office surveyor in the town. The Rev. A. B. Nicholls, Rector of Birr and husband of Charlotte Brontë, died in Banagher in 1906 but his wife had the good sense to seek inspiration for *Jane Eyre* from Eyrecourt, a small town six miles to the west.

There must, you may think, be some reason for visiting the place. There are three. First there is the quality of the cabbages which are the finest in the country. These are to be had at the draper's shop on the right-hand side of the main street as you walk up from the harbour. The second is the Crannog Pottery, run by Eyre Chatterton's cousin, Valerie Landon. This is a working studio pottery selling a great variety of handcrafts and I hope I will not be considered a complete philistine when I say that the best thing I ever purchased there was a pot of home-made marmalade. The third is Mick Hough's bar where the company is riotous, and the singing raucous, with Mick on guitar, his sister on piano and vocals, and the customers on stout poured by Mick's brother-in-law. Having boiled your cabbage, spread your marmalade and drunk your fill, Banagher will be an altogether different place to that which I have described.

We set off early next morning in an attempt to reach Portumna that year but were soon halted at Meelick because the lock did not open until eleven-thirty a.m. It was nine-fifty. Meelick, from the Irish Miliuc, means low marshy ground and at this point the Shannon is broken by a number of low islands, the watercourse being further complicated by the entry of the Little Brosna River. As a result of the shallows Meelick has long been a fording point and consequently the scene of much strife.

The Norman invasion of Ireland brought with it a great many adventurers who were more interested in building for themselves than in bearing allegiance to any crown across the sea. Among these people were the de Burgos and it was to them, through their marriage into important Irish families, that the saying "more Irish than the Irish" was first attributed. The family tree of the de Burgos— who were elevated to the Marquisate of Clanricarde in 1644—would fill a book on its own. In 1193 William de Burgo was granted the lands of Connacht and in 1203 he built a fort at Meelick. His son Richard built a stone fortress in 1229. We were to hear more of this family when we reached Portumna, but in the meantime we had no success in finding any remains of the early forts. On one of the wooded islands stand the Keelogue Batteries, opposite which there is a Martello tower, but these were erected at the same time as the Shannon Bridge defences.

SEVEN

Her Victorian Majesty

PORTUMNA LIES thirteen miles below Banagher, is as charmingly kept as Banagher is drab, and rivals Carrick as the most beautiful town on the river. Here there are tree-lined avenues of flowering cherry and the gardens are a riot of brightly-coloured flowers; we always remember the place as the town where even the reek of the turf stoves is made sweeter by the bouquet of the flowers hanging heavy in the still midland air. The houses and shops are in keeping with the gardens, and many of the shop fronts still sport the traditional painted corner stones and elegant lettered signs. One shop, Hayes and Son, Victualler, has a splendid wrought-iron canopy stretching across the pavement.

One suspects that the townspeople must be endowed with a good sense of humour since theirs is a town which has missed the tramp of progress in the most fickle manner. The town harbour lies at the end of a short length of canal but this stops short of the town itself by a good half mile. Even the railway, when it arrived in 1868, had its terminus on the opposite bank of the river. The route was never profitable and the line was closed after ten years, control returning from the railway company to the Public Works Commissioners. In 1883 they withdrew what staff remained. An estimated £20,000-worth of material was looted from the line almost overnight. The affair ended with a gang trying to spirit away a six-arch bridge over the River Brosna. The ill-fated line is now always referred to as "Portumna's stolen railway".

Shortly after we docked at Connacht Harbour, Portumna (Port Omna, the landing place of the oak) we were invited to lunch at a nearby restaurant by John Lefroy and his wife Sandra. John's family have long been associated with the river and John is manager of the Emerald Star base which lies along the canal. On our way across the bridge in John's car he admitted that he had a vested interest in our destination, the Ferry Inn, since he and his brother Tony, along with a friend in Dublin, were joint owners. Tony manages the establishment and from the succulent quality of the fair end of neck which we devoured that afternoon I can vouch that he manages well. It was the first of many mighty repasts we were to consume in the pleasant dining room overlooking the water and Portumna Bridge. Tony's only competition on that side of the river lies a few hundred yards down the road. There is no tradition of naming Irish bars but when the Lefroys expanded the premises to include the restaurant they decided to give the building the name of *The Ferry Inn*.

Almost overnight their neighbour erected a sign announcing *The Ferry Bar*. It was a canny move. As the Inn is well advertised throughout the town many people cross the bridge towards it, but the first premises they see are those of the Ferry Bar.

Just before we departed for Ireland we had seen on the front cover of *Motor Boat and Yachting* the photograph of a magnificent steam yacht. The caption just informed us that this was *Phoenix* on Lough Derg. It was with some surprise that we discovered her proud owners to be none other than John and Sandra and after lunch we set out for a tour of this grand old lady of the Shannon.

When John and Sandra bought *Phoenix* from John's father three years ago the original dinner gong was still in the inventory, although the vintage steam plant had been removed. Today she lies in the canal, among a bevy of glass-fibre craft whose stumpy lines only serve to enhance the elegance of what was once a gentleman's steam yacht and now represents one man's headache. John has his hands full throughout the summer patching up the result of many an over enthusiastic hirer's folly on what are described locally, and a little unfairly, as the "Tupperware" fleet. When there is a spare moment John is to be found sanding, varnishing, sawing or just gazing at Her Victorian Majesty, *Phoenix*, the most beautiful boat in all Ireland. That is John's story, and from the look in Sandra's eye it might just be true.

Phoenix was built by Malcolmson's of Waterford in 1873 for William Speight of Derry Castle on the shores of Lough Derg. She was built after the family home was destroyed by fire. And so *Phoenix* rose from the ashes – or, more accurately, the insurance money. She is a straight-stemmed, counter-stern yacht with a length of fifty-eight feet and a beam of ten feet six inches, displacing thirty-two tons. The quality of the Lowmor iron used was such that there has been little deterioration of the hull and although she is one of the oldest yachts registered with Lloyds there was no sign of trouble when she was dry-docked last year.

The Waterford shipbuilder's records were also destroyed by fire in the late nineteenth century, which makes discovery of her original statistics something of a detective hunt. Details of the steam plant are sketchy but, according to the entry at Lloyds, this consisted of a two-cylinder engine which achieved around fourteen horse-power. The boiler was housed beneath a magnificent teak and mahogany wheelhouse from which a companionway led forward to the main saloon at the head of which, perched on a plinth, stood the toilet. The throne room is still the original and is a neat bit of Victorian art with the handbasin hinging down on top of the pedestal. Behind the boiler, and separated from the stern cabin by an iron bulkhead, lies the engine room which now houses a 1961 Perkins diesel whose one hundred horse-power gives *Phoenix* a maximum speed of around ten knots. With her bow peaking to a knife edge, John often worries about coming across an erratically handled jelly mould boat at the wrong moment.

Bunkering a coal-fired boiler in the midlands of Ireland might well have been impossible, or at least highly expensive, since coal was generally only obtainable at the source of import. However, one of the few coal mines in the country lay on Lough Allen which was linked to the Shannon by canal. Each spring *Phoenix* made her way ninety miles upstream through Loughs Ree, Forbes, Bofin, Boderg, Tap and Corry to fill her bunkers which lined the engine room. Apart from the engine, *Phoenix* is slowly – John estimates the job will last a lifetime — being returned to her original splendour. In 1954 she was re-decked in pine and, says John, "God knows what else. I even found plywood." Originally the main deck alone was pine with teak on the poop and fo'c'stle. John has been forced to replace much of this with steel, which at least means she is water-tight above as well as below the waterline. It's a point of no little importance in Ireland. The wheelhouse, lost in 1954, has been replaced from old photographs. The stack behind the wheelhouse is the result of a search around the Guinness junk yard — the brewery is the parent company to Emerald Star — and many hours of welding. The hull, once white and then blue, has been returned to the original black.

So much for the technicalities. For those to whom boats are simply things round which yarns are wound, there are tales of *Phoenix* which are worthy of any contemporary monk's riverside annals. We were entertained to a number of these when we visited John and Sandra in their house by the canal. John produced a lemonade bottle containing an amber liquor but my hopes, and Val's fears, that I was about to sample the legendary poteen were dashed when Sandra explained that they had been to a point-to-point and having only a forty-ounce bottle available thought the soft drink container a more suitable decanter. Denied though I was of sampling the infamous distillation, I was not at a loss for a story about the stuff. On the previous day the sober columns of the *Irish Times* had carried news of some strange nocturnal exploits. Under the headline, "Poteen makers abandon still as Gardai sail in" a stirring tale was told.

It appears that a group of Connemara poteen makers were disturbed at their task by three members of the Gardai. The still was sited on the edge of an inland lake and the moonlighters immediately made off into the centre in a rowing boat, leaving their pursuers to run round in circles attempting to block their escape should they try to land. After a few hours one of the Gardai went off in search of another boat and reinforcements and on his return the amphibious posse set out in pursuit. The poteen makers dived over the side of their craft and swam to the shore, vanishing into the depths of a convenient bog. The newspaper report concluded with the information that twenty-two barrels of beer had been seized in the raid. I can only assume that somewhere in the bogs of Ireland there is a group of men who can perform miracles to equal any Bible story. Tales of converting water into wine pall at the thought of changing beer into the water of life.

It was not long before John's "lemonade" had loosened our tongues and we were soon swapping waterway yarns with the enthusiasm of old salts. John was the undoubted victor although I insist that he had an unfair advantage. *Phoenix*, after all, has been around a long time and she has pulled a good many tales in her wake.

In 1974 President Childers and his wife embarked at Banagher for the fourteen-mile trip north to the ancient religious settlement at Clonmacnois where the President was due to read a lesson at the annual Church of Ireland open-air ceremony. Time had been allowed for a stop along the way since the party was to have a picnic lunch. John sought advice from an old Shannon hand and then edged into the bank at the chosen point. He ran the bows up on an invisible rock. His adviser was quite unabashed and announced that it must be the only rock for miles. The hullabaloo was not decreased when one of the President's aides poked his head round the wheelhouse door and asked if the President was at the wheel at the time. The voyage continued peacefully enough, although little did the President know that John's absence from the wheel was because he was stuck in the engine room holding the oil pump on to its engine mounting.

The same year an American film unit, doing location work for a film on Irish emigration to the United States, hired *Phoenix* from John. The film was aptly titled *Give Us Your Poor*. *Phoenix* was stripped of her wheelhouse and other superstructure, equipped with two imitation paddles, and an enormous fluted stack. In order to create the impression of movement the special effects man produced a noxious chemical mixture which had the appearance of steam. This billowed forth for a while and then exploded with such a velocity that the stack was split like a banana. There is a splendid report of the film making in the *Irish Independent* which, beneath a photograph of the cast on board *Phoenix*, carries the caption: "Filming *Give Us Your Poof* On The Shores Of Lough Derg."

There is a sadder tale which dates from the days of the Black and Tans. In the middle of the bridge which spans the Shannon at Killaloe there is a tablet which commemorates in Irish the murder of four local lads at the hands of these infamous troops. There is a song about this tragedy which was collected by John's father Ian who heard it sung by a young girl in the town.

The dreadful news from Ireland spread,
It rang from shore to shore.
Of such a deed no living man
Has ever heard before.
And even Cromwell in his day
I'm sure no worse could do.
As they stand in court that murdered
Those poor boys in Killaloe.

'Twas on the 30th November, boys
That history will go down.
They were tracked and trailed from Galway
To a house in Williamstown.
They did not get a fighting chance,
They were captured while asleep,
And the way that they ill-treated them
Would cause your blood to creep.

They tied them up both hands and feet,
With thongs they could not break.
They brought them down to Killaloe,
By steamer on the lake.
Without clergy, judge or jury
On the bridge that night shot down.
And the blood flows with the Shannon
Convenient to the town.

If you were at their funeral —
It was a lovely sight —

To see one hundred clergymen
All robed out in white.
Their funeral at ten p.m. went through O'Gonnelloe,
The likes of those four martyrs in one grave lie below.
Young Rogers and McMahon,
Brave Egan and Kilday.

The "steamer" in the poem was *Phoenix*, which had been com-
mandeered by the troops.

Buying a comprehensive guide to those places in Ireland through
which the tourist buses do not pass is like finding a pint of stout on
Good Friday and we were grateful to John who introduced us to
Portumna's enthusiastic local historian, Dom Kearns. We met in
Dom's linoleum and oak-panelled premises in the main street but
since he had an hour to spare from his business — he is the town
solicitor and a busy man since, he informed us smilingly, small
rural communities are highly litigious — he escorted us to his house
nearby. Mrs. Kearns thought the occasion warranted the use of the
best silver. I have never seen a coffee percolator so large or so ornate
as that which was set forth on the table that morning. Mrs. Kearns
was called away to the telephone and bid us help ourselves to
coffee. But no one in the room had the courage to put a finger on
this mighty edifice. It also made a fine cup of coffee which is a rare
thing in Ireland where powdered sludge has conquered all before it.

Dom turned out to be a walking encyclopaedia of Portumna's
past and before we departed he pressed on us a copy of his home-
bound Portumna Scrapbook which covers the history of the town
and the surrounding area. It was from this that we gleaned much
of the story of the place which the official histories tend to omit.

The history of Portumna and the lands of Connacht which
surround it is inextricably tied up with the family who inhabited
the great fortified manor which overlooks Portumna Bay at the
northern end of Lough Derg. This building was gutted by fire in
1826, a fate which overtook its replacement in 1922. The stones of
the new building were re-dressed and used to construct the enormous Catholic church which dominates the town square. Today

the manor belongs to the State, along with the nearby church and Portumna Woods, and is the setting for a pleasant wildlife park. Board of Works scaffolding surrounds the building, known as Portumna Castle, and a restoration programme is well under way, although the memories which this will preserve are among the unhappiest in Ireland, since the owners of Portumna, the Clanricardes, were notorious landlords. The Castle sits apart from the wooded glades, its towering walls standing stark against the winds which howl across the lake. It is a chill and comfortless place, an architectural death mask with tiny unglazed windows set at regular intervals along the featureless squared walls and corner turrets. The roof-line is broken by a series of battlements and the entrances — there are only two — reveal the turbulent past of the place as they bristle with pistol loops and other defence mechanisms.

In 1566 Elizabeth's Ulster campaign encouraged her to establish plantations throughout Ireland and Sir Walter Raleigh's attempt in Munster was fairly successful, if the death of tens of thousands of natives is a measure of success. Edmund Spenser recorded the event with a poetic relish rather at odds with the nature of the proceedings: "Out of every corner of the woods and glens they came creeping forth upon their hands, for their legs would not bear them; they looked like anatomies of death; they spake like ghosts crying out of their graves." Yet the spirit of revolt was not stilled and in April 1599 Sir Robert Devereux, second Earl of Essex, Lord Lieutenant of Ireland and Elizabeth's current favourite, arrived with a force of seventeen thousand troops. His campaign was not decisive and the fallen idol was left to return to London and execution in 1601. That same year the Earl of Clanricarde died, Mountjoy besieged Kinsale, and Richard de Burgo (often known as Burgh or Burke) was knighted on the battlefield. It was he who built the fortified house at Portumna.

The fourth earl later married the luckless Earl of Essex's widow, Frances, who was the daughter of Elizabeth's highly successful spymaster, Sir Francis Walsingham. His good connections at Court, and his faithful service to the Queen, brought extensive favours. He became Governor of Connacht, a member of the privy council in Ireland, Viscount Tunbridge, and Baron of Somerhill, his Jacobean residence in Kent. In 1628 he received the titles of Viscount Galway and Earl of St. Albans. By 1632 however Sir Thomas Wentworth, later Earl of Strafford, was Lord Deputy of Ireland and he once again raised the threat of plantation. In 1635 he held an inquisition at Clanricarde's home for the purpose of declaring the lands of Connacht for the English Crown. At that time Clanricarde's revenue from the area was greater than that of the king. Wentworth had promised the juries that a large proportion of their lands would be left to them and had little difficulty in persuading them to concur with his wishes. The proceedings at Portumna were beset with problems but Wentworth, when that jury refused to agree with him, promptly escorted the members to Dublin where he convicted them in the Castle Chamber.

The Lord Deputy later noted in a State letter that he had thought "of a course to vindicate His Majesty's honour and justice". He then fined the Sheriff £1,000 and the jurors £400 each, sending them to prison "until the fines should be paid and until they should acknowledge their offence in court upon their knees". The Sheriff died in prison but according to an account in the *Irish Penny Magazine* of 1833 the jurors had their fines decreased and were "released at the solicitations of the Earl of Clanricarde". The Lord Deputy made preparations to summon another jury, but in the meantime Clanricarde died and his son Ulick accused Wentworth of hastening his father's death. The Lord Deputy replied with the accusation that both Richard and his son had illegally absented themselves from Ireland.

The Lord Deputy—Black Tom the Tyrant—went about his business and in 1637 another jury found for the Crown; the County of Galway was planted at a double rate and the natives lost half their lands instead of the normal quarter. Nevertheless a nineteenth-century account managed to conclude with a retrospective flourish: "The gentlemen of the county loudly proclaimed their discontent and fixed resolution to embrace any opportunity which might offer to be revenged, and of the sincerity of their determination the fatal events which later took place afforded melancholy proof."

In 1639 the Lord Deputy returned to England as Earl of Strafford but before he could do anything to protect Charles from his Parliamentary critics he found himself marching the well-trodden road to Tower Hill. Ironically one of the charges laid against him, although it was a Bill of Attainder which took him to the block, was that he acted tyrannically in Ireland. In 1641 the fifth earl returned to the Portumna estate and in October the rising began. Ulster fell and the Parliament in London passed the Adventurer's Act whereby Charles could no longer pardon rebels. The Act served later as the basis for Cromwell's Act of Settlement.

Ulick de Burgo was greatly favoured by Thomas Carte, the Jacobite preacher and historian whose defence of Charles I against the charge that he had instigated the massacre of 1641 caused him to flee to France. Carte's eulogy of the fifth earl found him to be "a man of great piety and strict virtue, regular in devotion, exemplary in life, considerate in all his actions". Carte also found him to possess "great natural talents" and one of these must have been an ability for self-preservation as he survived Cromwell's period in Ireland, assisting Inchiquin at the siege of Galway, and was Viceroy after Cromwell's departure. The Irish loyalists were less enthusiastic about the appointment and he returned to England in 1652 and died at Somerhill five years later. The fortunes of the de Burgos waxed and waned as king followed king, but in spite of finding themselves on the wrong side at Aughrim the family survived with their lands intact, thanks in part to the happy expedient of turning Protestant.

The last Marquess of Clanricarde succeeded in the twentieth century where Strafford had failed in the seventeenth. There are those in Portumna who remember the misery which the people of the estate endured at the hands of this cruel and tyrannical miser, the ultimate absentee landlord, who played with the destiny of his tenants from the safety of London until the British Parliament called an end to his outrageous behaviour.

He took over the estate on the death of his father, three years after Gladstone's Irish Land Act, the passing of which had caused him to resign as Member of Parliament for Galway. At this time the estate ran to fifty-two thousand acres with around two thousand tenants providing a yearly revenue of £25,000. The harvest of 1879 was the worst since the Great Famine but while many landlords either reduced their rents or put them into abeyance Clanricarde enforced his demands. A secret terror campaign called Captain Moonlight, swept rural communities and landlords and their agents were attacked. Clanricarde's agent Blake was suspected of encouraging his master to stand by his rent demands and was killed. But nothing worried the master who replied sardonically: "Do they think they will intimidate me by shooting my bailiffs?"

In 1886, with their rent standing at twenty-five per cent above the average, the tenants threatened to withhold payment. Clanricarde sent in the constables and seventy-five resisting tenants were imprisoned. Parnell encouraged the people with his Plan of Campaign whereby tenants who could not meet the landlord's demands paid what they could into a common fund which was given to the landlord if he met their request for a decrease in rent. If not, the cash was used for their defence in court. Boycotts of farmers who occupied evicted land, and of landlords themselves, were common and it was an Irish landlord, Captain Boycott, who thus enriched the English language.

Nothing could stop Clanricarde enforcing evictions; not the Chief Baron of the Court of Exchequer who proclaimed that the indignation of the Empire had been aroused by acts of Lord Clanricarde; not the Chief Secretary who refused the Marquess the forces of law to which he was entitled; not the English Liberals of the Home Rule Union, one of whom fought a superb case at law which spotlighted the inconsistencies of the courts which, with Gladstone's departure, were at liberty to sentence without benefit of trial by jury. In October 1887 Clanricarde sent in the sub-Sheriff with one hundred and fifty police, "and great opposition was offered by the tenants, hot water and stones were thrown on the bailiffs. In one case it took several hours to get possession and the police had to take the place with drawn swords."

In 1903 Wyndham's Act settled many of the injustices of land ownership with offers of mighty bonuses to landlords who gave up control. But it was not until 1909 that a Congested Districts Board was awarded the right to purchase the Clanricarde estate. The Marquess fought for six years against the ruling — in the Irish Rolls

Court, in the Court of Appeal, in the House of Lords and in the Irish Land Court. Eventually he was beaten, but not before he extracted £238,000 in compensation.

Remarkably, there is a happy sequel to these barbaric years, for on his death the house and demesne at Portumna came under the ownership of Henry Lascelles, eldest son of the fifth Earl of Harewood. Much was done to repair the old wounds and a plan to restore the old castle was commissioned though never undertaken. When Lascelles married Princess Mary the Clanricarde jewels were among her gifts and so was confirmed a two-hundred-year prophecy that one day these treasures would adorn the daughter of a king.

There was one moment in the Clanricarde purges which demands to be recorded more permanently. We found it among the notes of Monsignor Joyce, a former parish priest of Portumna who died in 1947, who had been working on a history of his native town. His papers are now in the possession of Dom Kearns and one of these records the trial of Wilfred Blunt, an English Liberal who came to Ireland to assist Clanricarde's tenants in their fight. He took part in a midnight meeting which was proclaimed and in spite of an appeal was sent to prison. The appeal was heard in Portumna in June 1888 and before it took place the citizens read an address, the eloquence of which is only equalled by Blunt's reply. The great speeches of Irish leaders are well quoted in the history books but this offering from the inhabitants of a tiny Irish town of which few people in England had heard is a magnificent oration which, along with the response, does much to account for the long memories one finds in Ireland. The introduction and conclusion are from Monsignor Joyce's notes.

In the morning before going to the courthouse the following address was presented to Mr. Blunt—Mr. P. J. Muldoon read the address—"We the people of Portumna beg to offer you our sincerest thanks for your disinterested championship of the poor on the Clanricarde property. Your efforts on behalf of suffering humanity in many quarters of the globe are of widespread notoriety. The people with whom you have so practically sympathised must have expressed their gratitude and we would be worse than ungrateful if we did not come forward and tender to you our deep and abiding love for the sacrifices you have made for us. In you we recognise a follower of the Grand Old Statesman, Mr. Gladstone, who had so generously devoted the autumn of his life to remedying the wrongs of centuries. In you we recognise an ambassador from the majority of the English people offering us the hand of friendship and bidding us to live in the hope of a justice long delayed. The hand you offer us we grasp in all sincerity. For years the anti-Irish Press had the ears of the world and we were represented at home and abroad as the very Hottentots Lord Salisbury described us, fit only to be the hewers of wood and drawers of water. But a bright ray shone through the darkness which surrounded the Castle rule when justice-loving Englishmen like you, from personal observation, drew the eyes of your countrymen on the enormity of the wrongs inflicted on a long-suffering people by heartless landlords and cruel misgovernment.

"We may have to wait a little for freedom, we may have to suffer with patience as becomes a noble people who though often defeated are never conquered. Our leaders may be imprisoned, the homes of our people may be levelled, but our voices shall never be silenced by the proclamation of our enemies. We have confidence in Mr. Parnell and in our trusted leaders and strong in that confidence we shall fight fearlessly and crimelessly for the righting of every Irish wrong, and of that self-government of which we were shamelessly robbed. You have ever been the champion of the justice which we seek. When history comes to be written the name of Wilfred Scawen Blunt shall be handed down to what we hope will be a free and prosperous people, as the name of a good man willing to sacrifice his own liberty on the altar of justice and freedom. And if your liberty is sacrificed our gratitude and affection follow you to your prison cell and our sympathy strong as Irish hearts can feel is the solace we offer your devoted wife whilst you are being martyred in the cause of the suffering poor."

Mr. Blunt in reply said: ". . . my visit to Portumna is made under exceptional circumstances—at least exceptional for an

In search of Kincora. A safe mooring in the old canal cut which led from Killaloe to Limerick before the river levels rose to accommodate the hydro-electric scheme. The narrow wall makes a good mooring but is a nasty catwalk on a dark evening.

A barge rally at Shannon Harbour. The ivy-clad ruin of the former Canal Company hotel towers incongruously above the wharf.

The Grand Canal Company stores, Athlone, in 1936.

Title page from James Dawson's pamphlet recommending canal extensions in 1819.

CANAL EXTENSIONS
IN IRELAND,

RECOMMENDED

TO THE IMPERIAL LEGISLATURE,

AS

THE BEST MEANS OF

Promoting the Agriculture—Draining the Bogs—and Employing the Poor,

OF

IRELAND;

AND ALSO,

AS THE SUREST MEANS OF

SUPPLYING THE BRITISH MARKETS WITH CORN,

REDUCING THE RATES OF FOREIGN EXCHANGES,

AND

FACILITATING THE GENERAL RESUMPTION OF CASH PAYMENTS.

BY JAMES DAWSON, ESQ.

Dublin:

PRINTED BY WILLIAM PORTER, GRAFTON-STREET.

1819.

Englishman – but it is not exceptional for an Irishman to have to appear in law courts on charges connected with political matters. When I learned two years ago the facts about the evictions of the Clanricarde Estate I came to Galway to show my sympathy with the people. The family which the present Lord Clanricarde represents, the Burkes, is quite the oldest Norman family in Ireland. It is very sad to find the present representative of that Irish family which was so closely connected with history and liberty in Ireland for many centuries so antagonistic to the interests and rights of the people . . . I would like to remind you of the history of Portumna in Charles I's days. The people here in Portumna broke the power of Lord Strafford who sought to take the lands from the people. Your forefathers were brave and uncompromising; their struggle ought to encourage you in your present land struggle."

Cordons of police were drawn across the streets when Mr. Blunt left the court. Hearty cheers were given again and again by the crowd as the prisoner · walked to Keary's Hotel. The Portumna Brass Band played "God Save Ireland" and sought to get near the hotel but were dispersed by the police who charged with rapid pace to execute the order Clear The People Off The Roads. The band however continued to play some of the National airs and a collision was averted only by the intervention of the priests and other influential leaders. The traders in the town displayed their sympathy by closing their shops and shuttering their doors and windows. In the private houses the blinds were drawn, in some cases mourning bands were placed on the doors.

The carriage bearing Mr. Blunt to Galway Jail left Portumna at two o'clock under a heavy escort of fully armed police in charge of District Inspector Wade. As the car sped on its way deafening cheers were given by vast crowds who lingered in the streets to tender their farewell to the distinguished prisoner.

In the nineteenth century Louisa Beaufort visited Portumna Castle and though it is hard to imagine, from the stark shell which remains, that this place was once a richly-furnished house, her diary account of the interior shows that here indeed were the very rich

8

beds upon which Wentworth had the audacity to cast himself without removing his riding boots, an event which enraged Ulick de
Burgo. According to Miss Beaufort's memory

> the ceiling is rich and heavy, not coloured, the wainscot, dark
> red—beyond it is a breakfast room, and my Lord's dressing
> room and other chambers—they are all fitted up in the most
> appropriate castle style and there are several family pictures . . .
> the panels of the lower half of the window shutters looking glass
> —which had a beautiful effect—there is a fine view of the
> Shannon.

Only the view of the Shannon remains constant in this place of
change and turmoil, but there is one small epitaph to the family
who brought both pain and pleasure to the inhabitants of Portumna.
Not all the Clanricardes were imbued with the foul spirit of the
last of their line. As we circled the house we came upon a protruding
window beneath which there is an engraved tablet. It is something
of an ironic memorial for it is not some dead and gloried Clanricarde
who is remembered but a pet dog:

This stone was erected to the Memory of a much lamented Animal
Who with a beauteous form possessed
Those qualities which are esteemed
most valuable in the human species:
Fidelity and Gratitude.
And Dying April 20th 1797, Aged 11 years
Was interred near this place.
Alas poor Fury
She was a Dog take her All in All
Eye shall not look upon her like again.

A few yards from Portumna Castle are the remains of a Dominican
friary, the buildings dating from the fifteenth century. The time-
worn richly hued stones of the cruciform building lying amid
green lawns and neat paths make a pleasant retreat after the over-
bearing aspect of the castle. The choir was still roofed as late as

1810 and in use as the Protestant parish church under, I believe, the Clanricardes' curate.

Having steeped ourselves in the history of this place we were only too pleased to seek out a path which Dom had described to us and we were soon on a forest road which led into the cool depths of Portumna Woods. The area abounds with sixteen species of Ireland's wild mammals, from the smallest pygmy shrew to the second largest, the fallow deer. You need a quick eye to catch sight of more than the rumps of the latter as they zig-zag defensively away from your scent. They have a great fear of the human species. Also to be found in the woods, although you are unlikely to see one, is the rarest of them all, the pine marten. The Forest and Wildlife Service have created a beautiful walk through the estate and a brief guide was available. Most of us can identify an oak from an ash but there were a number of stops on the trail which would have remained a mystery without this helpful booklet.

We had seen many references to turloughs but had no idea as to what they were until we arrived at an open glade in the wood. In Irish the word is *tur loch*, a dry lake. In winter it provides a feeding ground for mallard and teal while in summer the dried-out bed provides good grazing. These winter lakes are to be found in many limestone areas, particularly in the west of Ireland. The depressions have subterranean drainage systems and because their floors are so near permanent water, they tend to flood in wet weather. Further along the trail we came across something which I suspect would stump the most enthusiastic naturalist. It was a "mineral lick" containing trace elements of calcium, iron, salt, zinc and magnesium. Male deer require enormous quantities of calcium and phosphorus to help them grow new antlers and in order to reduce forest damage by bark stripping, from which these trace elements are usually acquired, this instant bark has been provided.

Having completed a circular walk of just over a mile we arrived back at the lakeside and searched in vain for some promised cormorants. Although we had often seen these large birds diving for their prey off the west coast of Scotland and Ireland, we had never before supposed that they frequented fresh water. Lough Derg is a rare inland breeding ground. We did feel that the forest guide's way of directing your gaze to the cormorants' favourite island was a masterly piece of copy writing: ". . . the white colouration which you may see on the pine trees is caused by . . ." I shall leave you to complete the sentence.

It was two days since we had felt the throb of *Fenniscourt*'s engines beneath our feet and it was time to say goodbye to Portumna and our friends. The course lay south into Lough Derg but first we had to negotiate the swing arch of Portumna Bridge. In 1795 an Act of Parliament decreed that a bridge should be built across the Shannon at Portumna. It was a toll bridge provided with one rising portcullis to enable ships to pass through. A wooden structure was erected the following year by an American architect called Cox. It was almost eight hundred feet in length and consisted of a number of arches, one of which lay on an island in mid-stream. The great flood of 1814 destroyed that part of the bridge on the Galway side and it was four years before a permanent repair was made to the wooden structure.

The present metal bridge is less likely to collapse in any flood but it is highly inconvenient to both road and river users since nothing larger than a dinghy can pass through without the swing arch being opened. Until a few years ago this was a laborious process since the bridge-keeper, who lives in a pleasant cottage on the island, was obliged to perform this service by means of a vast hand-operated capstan. Today the four-hundred-ton swing arch is opened by an electric winch but this has not greatly increased the speed of the operation. Boatmen usually keep their heads down while this cumbersome affair rumbles open, since, if looks could sink you, those on the faces of the drivers of the long line of cars which always builds up along the road surely would. Of course there is never a car to be seen when no boat wants to pass through.

EIGHT

In Search of Kincora

Oh where, Kincora, is Brian the great!
Oh, where is the beauty that once was thine!
Oh, where are the princes and nobles that sate
At the feast in thy halls, and drank the red wine?
Where, oh, Kincora?

WHERE INDEED lies Kincora, headquarters of the legendary Brian Boru? That poem was written by MacLiag, who was elevated to be the chief poet of Erin, and translated by James Clarence Mangan. It was written as a lament after Brian's death on the battlefield of Clontarf. It tells us nothing of the whereabouts of Brian's castle, but, although the location has long been a matter of dispute, there are many who claim that it occupied the site of the Catholic church which lies on the hill at the top of the main street of Killaloe. Perhaps the true castle has yet to be discovered, and when it is, no doubt some enterprising farmer will have converted it into a byre for his cattle..

In search of Kincora, Ceann-coradh, the head or hill of the weir, we set *Fenniscourt*'s bows in the direction of Killaloe. And if we did not find any sign of the stronghold of this Shannon king, we came away with enough myths and legends to provide a richer tapestry for thought than any cold historical account would provide.

First we had to traverse Lough Derg, longest and southernmost of the Shannon lakes. The scenery along the twenty-five-mile route from Portumna to Killaloe is more inspiring than any other stretch of Shannon water but the lake, as a result of the many arms which lead off from the main channel, and the gorges which penetrate the mountains, allowing the wind to whirl down on the unsuspecting boatman, is very prone to sudden squalls. Little surprise then that this should be Lough Dergdherc, the lake of the red eye. The eye of many a Shannon storm is centred here. But that is not the reason for this naming of the lake. For that we must turn once more to the stories of Ireland when the druids had their colonies on the islands and the poets and seers strode the country, honoured and feared even by kings.

One day a poet came to visit a king who lived by the shores of the lake, and when the court enquired as to what gift would be most suitable for such a learned man, the poet demanded the eye of the king. The king was old and had lost an eye in battle, but nevertheless he plucked his eye from its socket and presented it to his guest. Then the king was helped to the waters of the Shannon and they turned crimson. When the king was told of this he named the lake Dergdherc.

But the only crimson on the waters of the lake as Val took the helm and set us on a course by Gortmore Point and into the first long strait by which one navigates south, was the fiery reflection of the sun on silver water. Lough Derg was in a friendly mood, her frequent curtain of cloud and storm parted to reveal a backdrop of shoreline majesty. After our hearty walks through Portumna Woods and long lively nights at the Ferry Inn it was grand to relax, roll back the cockpit roof, and watch the perfect crest of the bow wave strive to complete a crescent from shore to shore.

The vista before us narrowed as we passed Split Rock and the entrance to Rossmore Bay, where an isolated jetty makes a pleasant mooring at the mouth of the Woodford River. Before us lay Illaunmore (Oileannmor: big island) and then the Carrigeens (little rocks). But it was to the shore that our attention was drawn, first to the west where the mighty range of Slieve Aughty rises to more than one thousand feet and then to the east where the more distant but higher peaks of the Slieve Blooms contain Arderin, the height of Erin (1,734 feet). But this was not to be the most spectacular moment. That came as we turned west, with *Fenniscourt* in mid-channel, Hare Island to starboard and the delightful harbour of Garrykennedy with its ruined quayside castle outlined against the trees to port. Beside us the Arra Mountains and Tountinna rose abruptly on the Tipperary shore and beyond them, just visible in the haze, Slievekimalta – Keeper Hill – etched its 2,279 feet across the skyline. And as we rounded Parker Point and headed into the narrow arm which leads to Killaloe, the peaks massed above us and the sun vanished behind Slieve Bernagh, the mountain of the gap. Now we were left to complete our voyage in the cool early gloaming one might expect in a coastal fiord, and it would have been easy to imagine that round the next corner we would meet the broad swell of the Atlantic.

This is the Shannon's most unusual feature, for here we have a river which, after tumbling from its mountain source, passes through a broad sweeping plain only to pass through yet another mountain area before its final fall to salt water. Time was when the Shannon poured out of Lough Derg over a natural rock sill at Killaloe and a canal threaded its way in and out of the river to the sea at Limerick. Since Ardnacrusha power station was built the land below Killaloe has been flooded. Passage to the sea is still possible through two enormous automatic locks in the heart of the power station, but since the course of the new route runs between high concrete ledges, over which the crew of a boat cannot see, we had decided to make Killaloe the limit, but not the end, of our Shannon journey. It is also the limit of navigation for hire cruisers.

The marina which lies on the opposite bank from Killaloe, in the village of Ballina, was packed with craft but just before we reached the buoyed channel which leads to the bridge, we noticed a low concrete wall running parallel to the bank making a channel some thirty feet wide. This was the line of the old canal, which is still navigable for some way on either side of the now disused Killaloe lock. A number of craft were moored to this old dyke which separated the canal from the river and we passed between two white posts which mark the entrance and made fast to two convenient iron rings. Our pleasure at finding a quiet mooring so near the town was to be spoiled later that evening after a pleasant amble around the hostelries of Killaloe. The wall is less than a foot wide and while passage along it is quite simple when there are craft moored on the canal side, the gaps between these craft, when we found ourselves walking a kind of tightrope with a fast running river on one side and a sheer drop into a deep canal on the other, was more than my head could take. Thankfully, it was dark, and no one observed my four-legged return to *Fenniscourt*.

In the morning we were better able to appreciate this jewel of the Shannon. The lake narrows to become river again and where the river narrows to twist under the bridge the crags on the Killaloe shore overhang the water. There is just enough room for a narrow road and a few houses to run parallel with the water, the houses facing the road and their backs only a few feet from the cliff face. A path leads upwards and at one point you actually pass the first and second floor windows. From our vantage point we looked down on the bridge where the opening of the co-operative creamery had caused a miniature traffic jam as local farmers arrived on tractors, their precious churns banging around on trailers. Beyond them we could see the line of the old railway and the Victorian red brick station standing like an island in the middle of the grassed tracks. The station is now a house and tourist information centre.

Killaloe is known in Irish as Cill Dálua, the church of St. Dálua, sometimes called Molua and frequently abbreviated to Lua. As we came to the top of this cliff path and out on to the road which led back to town, we entered a square surrounded by old houses. In the centre stood the usual vast Catholic parish church, the proportions of which would have better suited central London. In spite of its bulk and the height of its tower the church cannot be seen from the river and, in fact, due to the sharp elevation of the surrounding roads, it does not capture the eye of the traveller from any distance. This sheer-sided memorial to a pugnacious form of Christian archi-tecture looks all the more ridiculous since in the same churchyard lies the tiny Oratory of St. Lua.

The quiet eloquence of this building, with its stone-roofed chancel, speaks of an age when man was more humble in his worship of his God and the sign inside, which reminds visitors that this is a Holy Place, seemed singularly unnecessary. The Oratory was moved

to this site in 1929, under the supervision of the Irish antiquarian
R. A. S. MacAlister, when the Shannon Scheme flooded Friars
Island on which it had originally been constructed. On the other
side of the churchyard a single gravestone caught our attention. It
was a memorial to a group of children who had been drowned in the
canal at Killaloe. We were to see many similar stones on our journey
along the Grand Canal.

Coming down the long main street Val and I noticed that Killaloe
is one of these Irish towns where no two shops seem to open at the
same time on the same day. Throughout our stay here the place
had an air of never quite waking up. Eventually we did manage to
prise a grocer from his bed and he was quite happy to replenish our
stores, throwing in some fresh garden greens while he was at it.
As he said, it wouldn't be worth buying if it wasn't local. To which
I felt inclined to retort that anything would be worth buying if only
the shops would open.

Where the road along the river winds inland, separated from the
river by a bank of woodland, we found another tiny stone-roofed
building, the nave of St. Flannan's Church. The door and arch,
which would have led into the rest of this building, have been closed
with metal grids and we could but peer into the murky depths where
a number of stone objects were stored. The building lies in the
grounds of St. Flannan's Cathedral, attributed to King Donal Mor O
Brien, built in the twelfth century, and much modified since. We
knew that the shaft of a cross, remarkable for its Runic and Ogham
inscriptions, lay somewhere about the church and since a gardener
was tending the hedges I enquired as to where I could find this
monument. I would hardly have thought that Killaloe was inundated
with visitors making their way in droves in search of ancient bits of
stone, but the scowl on the gardener's face when he heard my
request seemed to indicate that this was the hundredth time that
day he had been asked. Without ceasing from his labours he muttered that he was just the gardener and didn't go in for such things.

It was the first and last time on our journey we met such un-
helpfulness. In the end we had the last laugh since our bad-tempered
gardener had left the keys in the church door. Removing them just
in case he had any bright ideas about locking us in for the night –

the souls of dead saints are not my idea of bedtime company – we entered.

Killaloe's ancient stone does not exactly leap up at you but it is historically precious, since there are few examples of Runic inscription in Ireland and none with Ogham writing as well. Ogham was the earliest form of writing known in Ireland and it originated there. The alphabet consists of a number of strokes set at different points along a central line. It was a limited and unwieldy form of writing, but, although it was quickly replaced by Latin script, the art did not entirely die out and there is one curious account of its use as late as the nineteenth century.

We came across this in one of the most endearing celebrations of Ireland and the Irish ever written. Robert Lloyd Praeger was a botanist of distinction and he took part in many archaeological investigations. After many years of "quiet wandering on foot along brown streams and among the windy hills" of Ireland Mr. Praeger put his observations into *The Way That I Went*. If the book astounds by the amount of ground it covers—and its author must have had sore feet by the end of it – it further amazes the reader by its attention to detail, all recorded in an elegant romantic style, so that the problem of crossing rivers without a bridge becomes a difficulty "owing to the superfluity of water in Ireland" which results "in a plethora of broad ditches and anastomosing swamps of lakes".

The solution to this difficulty?

One could flounder across using both arms and legs, wishing that coiling pond weeds did not lead to such Laocoon-like struggling. Or as you hesitate on the edge of a twenty-foot drain, a friendly hay-maker in the next meadow will hail you: "Ye'll fin' a foot-stick down beyant the fince", and you weather five formidable fences to reach a wobbly fir-trunk thrown across from bank to bank, so slippery that it would puzzle a tight-rope walker to negotiate it.

Having forded the Shannon at Killaloe, Mr. Praeger came to the ancient stone there and while recording in proper detail the importance of this relic he also managed to slip in "the startling fact that so late as the nineteenth century a farmer called Collins, living near the old Head of Kinsale, was prosecuted by the police for not having his name duly inscribed on his cart; but it was there — in Ogham."

Apart from the shaft of the cross with its strange writing, the simple interior of the cathedral contains one other item of note; a many-tiered Romanesque doorway, added from some other building, and used here as a window. We were to see a finer example of this type of architecture when we visited the cathedral at Clonfert later on our voyage.

Having taken our fill of historical stimulation it was time to search for some liquid refreshment and, with one accord so to speak, we set out across the bridge to the Lakeside Hotel where we promised ourselves something cool and black with a head of cream. And at the end of it all there was another undignified crawl along the dyke. The sky had been cloudless throughout the day but in spite of the chill in the air, the moon and the stars cast such a silver glow across the mountain ridges which surrounded our mooring that we sat on deck until long past midnight talking about the stories we had heard in the bar. The Lakeside Hotel is one of those hostelries where you may chat with a complete stranger for the entire evening and never find the need to introduce yourself. There was one gentleman there that evening who, hearing of our journey, decided to impart the entire history of Ireland in the space of a few short hours. But at last we were able to direct the conversation to the fabled mountains round Killaloe, to the days of Kincora and the deeds of Brian Boru. And before long he was quoting us more of the poem by the King's bard.

> They are gone those heroes of royal birth,
> Who plundered no church, who broke no trust;
> 'Tis weary for me to be living on earth
> When they, oh, Kincora, lie now in the dust!
> Low, oh, Kincora.

Kincora may have gone, and the heather wine with it, but the quality of Ireland's native beverage lives on to inspire the stories of the past. We have never come across any accounts of people walking on the waters of the Shannon but there was a fable with a definite Biblical ring told that evening. It concerned the voyage of an ancient people who came from the Nile, having been told that in Ireland lay their only refuge from the flood. It seems that there were three boatloads of women with only two men to assist them and when, on reaching Ireland, one of the men died, the survivor, Fintan the Deathless, was so overcome by the demands of the womenfolk that he fled to the heights of Tountinna. And when the flood came the women perished and Fintan was saved. It is a fine watery tale and quite suitable entertainment for a Shannon voyage – even if I did discover later that it is a rather heavily adapted version of a story which appears in the *Book of Invasions*.

There is another story about this mountain. It concerns Gorm-flath, wife of the Norse King Olaf. After Olaf's defeat Gormflath became Malachy's wife, and later she was to marry Brian Boru himself. She was known as the woman who did all things ill over which she had any power. The King of Leinster was greatly captivated by one of Brian's daughters but Gormflath would have none of this and, without Brian's knowledge, sent a detachment of her husband's troops to ambush the Leinster king on his way to Kincora. The site is marked to this day on the Ordnance Survey map as the Graves of the Leinster Men. Alas for the writers of fable, the slate slabs which mark the spot have been attributed to the Bronze Age and whatever may lie beneath them it is not the bones of the Leinster men.

The following morning the water in the sheltered narrows at Killaloe was restless. As we were about to leave the security of our canal moorings, we heard that a cruiser had run aground and was badly holed at Aughinish Point, seven miles back up Lough Derg at one of the most treacherous parts of the navigation. In the original Irish Aughinish, Each-inis, means the island of horses and there were plenty of white ones in the narrow channel which leads out of this arm of Lough Derg between the Lushing Rocks and the Tully Rocks. The confusion of the seas was not helped by the appearance of an express cruiser, planing along somewhere in the region of twenty knots, which passed with a wave from the skipper and a wake like the Severn Bore.

We were now in that part of the lake where the arm from Killaloe meets Scarriff Bay to the west and the long stretch of water leading past Garrykennedy to Youghal Bay in the east. Derg on a wild day is at its wildest here as the famous Scarriff Breeze rips across the lake and piles up highly unpleasant box waves. The effect of all this on *Fenniscourt* was that no matter in which direction I pointed the bows, we rolled and yawed wildly as the fixed sides of the high central cockpit caught the wind like a sail. I was perched on a free-standing high seat as *Fenniscourt* met the full effect of the wind. In something approaching lunatic foolhardiness I had one hand resting gently on the wheel, the front feet of the stool off the ground, and my back wedged against the open cockpit door. For a split second, as the first wave hit the beam, I found myself soaked and suspended in mid-air, the stool clattering to the deck. Being unable to master the art of levitation I followed the stool, grabbing as I did so the lever which decompressed and stopped the engine. The language which was heard at that moment would have put a God-fearing man in the confession box for a week.

While I was working out which part of my body most ached, Val, who had been attempting to get the neck of a brandy bottle to hover somewhere near the rim of a glass, emerged from the saloon. "I think that there's a rock outside," she said, with a measure of composure which would have done justice to Moby Dick. "We can outrun the wind and the storm," wrote John Burroughs, "but we cannot outrun the demon of hurry." I have news for Mr. Burroughs. We outran the lot. The rock turned out to be a black buoy but it might as well have been a reef, since it marked the beginning of the Shannon's nastiest underwater hazard, the Middle Ground. With her engine silent *Fenniscourt* was drifting and would soon lie neatly between the black and red buoys which is just where you should be at any point on the Shannon other than the Middle Ground. The engine caught at the first turn of the key, which I am happy to say that it did throughout our voyage, and I brought her bows round and out of danger.

The Middle Ground is only rivalled by the Benjamin Rocks, the marked channel between which I have never been able to fathom, as the most confusing part of the navigation. The shoal, hidden throughout the year, is marked by two red buoys to the north and two black buoys to the south. The markers are painted with signs announcing Middle Ground N.W. and Middle Ground N.E. and so on but "if you can read this you are too close", as the motorists' sticker says. The passage round the obstacle is to the north of the red buoys or to the south of the black buoys, which is in direct contradiction to all other marked channels.

The names of the Shannon rocks and shoals should be a timely warning to any mariner for many owe their title to a craft which foundered on them. Billy English told us that Galey Bay on Lough Ree had been a favourite area for regattas in the nineteenth century and that the Louisa Shoal which lies across its mouth was so named when the commodore's yacht ran aground here.

> To Hodson's Bay our course we bent,
> The *Sylph* and others followed after.
> To gain the prize was our intent,
> The *Adelaide* provoked some laughter.
>
> As down along the Shannon's side
> Our yacht *Louisa* easy sailing,
> The *Adelaide* still strove to shade
> From us the breeze then light prevailing.

The tricks of the *Adelaide*, commemorated in that extract from a poem in *Louisa*'s log which Billy estimates as having been written in August 1833, were to be her undoing and Adelaide Rock, west of Inchmore, marks the spot where she ran out of water. Slate Rock, which appears above water level every summer and was a problem in the old days before it was marked, got its name from a slate-carrying barge which ran aground there.

With these thoughts to cheer us we regained an albeit shaky degree of control and Val vanished once more below decks. "There's nought, no doubt, so much the spirit calms, as rum and true religion." If you cannot get rum, brandy will suffice. Dispensing with glasses, two of which, I was informed, had come to grief while I was performing my acrobatics around the cockpit, I gave thanks to the French and drank to the Jacobites. I also spent the rest of the journey standing rather than sitting. I thought Val's suggestion that she lash me to the wheel a trifle extreme.

There was no sign of a wrecked cruiser, although *Fenniscourt* at that moment might have passed for a near miss. Through the binoculars however Val sighted what appeared to be the stern of a boat heading fast round the wooded knoll of Hare Island and, sweeping the lake, she spotted another craft crawling along well in its wake. Opening the throttle we came abreast of this mystery vessel although she was a good mile off to port. Through the glasses we could see the stocky snub-nosed outline of an old canal barge fairly bludgeoning her way through the sharp seas. We now lay equidistant between the barge and Garrykennedy and since I thought the feeling of the good green earth beneath my feet would do much to restore my sense of well-being we peeled off for that welcome haven.

The man who engineered the harbour at Garrykennedy had a great sense of humour. It is a fine poem in stone and mortar, with the remnants of an ancient keep adding a touch of distinction. It would appear to be contemporary with other harbours built in the early nineteenth century but it is so designed as to be accessible only to those who have passed some sort of Mensa test in seamanship. First there is a filthy-looking shoal to the west of the entrance. Then there is a nasty rock to the east. Both are well marked but once you have entered this narrow channel there is no retreat. You must get into the harbour before you can turn. The stone-walled entrance is narrow, a bare thirteen feet I should think, and there's a kink in it. Once inside the high walls you find that the only steps giving access to the quay, unless you are of Brobdingnagian proportions and fancy a leap from the cabin roof, lie on one side. The wind that day took *Fenniscourt* to every side of the harbour except the one with the steps. To make matters worse – and you cannot get much worse than this – somebody's proud new bright yellow Microplus day-boat lay moored in one corner and it was with the greatest difficulty that I avoided topping someone's new bright yellow Microplus like an egg.

Our ballet dance around the harbour, although perhaps it was more akin to a street fight sequence from *West Side Story*, drew the attentions of a lady who lived in a nearby cottage. She stood on the quay shaking her head in disbelief or disgust and just as Val was about to cast her a rope, the good lady fled indoors. No doubt the waterway telegraph would be transmitting news of our ungainly arrival. To this day I do not know how we managed to secure a line ashore.

But dry land was dry land, and we were thankful for it. Looking back towards the lake to see where the barge had gone, we were astonished to see her lying about fifty yards offshore, her anchor down, and the crew approaching the harbour in the dinghy. Whoever her skipper was he knew a thing or two about Shannon moorings, since the combination of the wind and the nearby rocks made his anchorage look precarious. As the dinghy drew towards the shore we made out the bearded figure of none other than John Lefroy.

After introducing us to the skipper of the barge, Geoff Tottenham, and his wife, John explained that one of his boats had grounded the previous evening and, unable to do anything as darkness fell, they had rescued the crew and summoned Geoff and the good ship *Venus* to help pull her off in the morning. There followed a brief debate as to which of Garrykennedy's two hostelries we should favour with our custom but we were soon heading in the direction of the bar called Cissy's. Not a great deal happens in Garrykennedy on a weekday and our arrival in Cissy's parlour caused a moment of consternation as she sought the key for the bar. Once ensconced we all set about righting the various wrongs of the morning. John and Geoff had spent a tough hour or so rescuing the marooned boat and I had a number of bashes and bangs which required some internal tranquillising.

John assured everyone that he would only be stopping for a short while, but Irish time is a little like Irish miles – it lasts as long as those who pass through it wish it to continue. Each of the gentlemen in the company had to buy a round, and then each of us had to insist on buying the last one. That made six rounds. As the rounds continued so also did a conversation on the merits of boats and messing about on them. And in the course of this merry afternoon Geoff told us one of the finest "true stories" of the days when the Grand Canal barges used to ply the length of Lough Derg from Portumna to Killaloe.

The *St. James* was a Shannon tug which used to tow the barges across the lake. Often a string of four or five barges would cross in this manner and one day a private yacht appeared and asked, as the skipper thought his engine a bit dicky, if they might tag along. The master agreed and the flotilla went on its way. But it wasn't long until the skipper of the yacht hailed the last barge to which he was tied.

"Say there," says the skipper, "how in the name of all that's holy is it that we're making so little way, with the *St. James* going full ahead and all the barges going full ahead?"

"Sure the *St. James* is going full ahead and a very nice bit of power she's putting on it is. And that's no problem at all," came the reply. "But the trouble is that there's a dance on tonight in Mountshannon and as you well know, sir, we've had a long haul getting here from Dublin and it'll be a long haul back and Mountshannon's half way to Killaloe, sir. So the *St. James* can go ahead as fast as she likes but we're going full astern and I think we've just got the edge on her. So we'll just make it to Mountshannon by nightfall. It'll be a fine dance, sir, so I suggest you join the party."

Throughout the proceedings Geoff would peer from the window of the bar to ensure that the *Venus* was still afloat and that sufficient filthy smoke was coming from the exhaust to indicate that the ancient, temperamental and, from an engineer's point of view, miraculous original Bolinder engine was behaving itself. The wind had slackened while we were enjoying ourself in Cissy's and when the time came to wave John and his friends goodbye, the sun was making inroads in the clouds.

NINE

Bars and Bards

WITH THE LAKE settling to the kind of dead calm which can appear as suddenly as any storm, we resumed our interrupted journey to the harbour of Mountshannon, tucked away in the bay of the same name and hidden from the outer lake by a string of islands; Inish-parran, which is more of a bulbous peninsula linked to the main-land by a narrow causeway, Cribby Islands, Bushy Island, Young Island and the largest of them all, the legendary Inis Cealtra, the Holy Island of Lough Derg, with its round tower or Clogás climbing upward for eighty feet from the slopes of the island's green-backed hump.

By the time we had moored inside the harbour the evening was upon us and we decided to leave our exploration of Lough Derg's monastic remains until the following day. The village of Mount-shannon rests where the foothills of the Slieve Aughty Mountains turn the map brown to the very shores of the lake, and, as a result, you ascend to the village proper by way of a hill road bound on each side by high, wild hedgerows.

The main road from Portumna passes through the village, running along the flood plain to Scarriff and Killaloe, but like many Irish roads it is little used and does nothing to disturb the peace of the place. Single-storey cottages line the street and open directly on to the pavement, but still the flowers survive, thrusting their way through the pavement and rambling over trellises. There are palms here, and in front of one of the cottages there is a splendid array of arum lilies poking their way incongruously through the tar.

No doubt the islands across the mouth of Mountshannon Bay shelter the village from the worst of the Scarriff Breeze and this would account for the abundance of sweet-smelling blooms and fine trees which line the highway. The village has the usual crop of grocery bars and it was in one of these that we took the weight off our feet while the proprietor went about the business of replenishing *Fenniscourt*'s stores. He went so far as to provide us with a trolley on which to convey them to the quay, insisting that we left it there to be collected by his son. With a prayer to Inis Cealtra's patron, Saint Caimin, that he might still the wind and the waves on the following day, we doused *Fenniscourt*'s lights and hit the hay.

The cows which graze the rich pasture of Inis Cealtra were all upstanding next morning as we approached the tiny quay on the northern shore, and, unless they worked for the Meteorological Office, it looked like being a fine, though slightly windy day. Beside the quay stood a stone shack, hardly an ancient relic in spite of the crane hanging over the blackened hearth, but a shelter for the boatmen who used to convey the pilgrim visitors. The island appears in the journal of an Irish tour in 1680: "This is two small miles about in the Shannon River . . . called the Seven Churches of Asia. Here once a year the superstitious Irish go to do penance, and are enjoined to walk round bare-footed seven times, and they who fear hurting their feet hire others to do it." Salvation by proxy would seem to have been the order of the day if our ancient chronicler is to be believed, but we found it hard to understand how anyone could find the least discomfort walking the gentle swards of Inis Cealtra.

Heading inland we stood among the ruins with their memories of Ireland's early monasticism, of St. Patrick and St. Columcille, or St. Columba as he was later to be known on that other holy island of Iona. I do not know if any of these famous saints ever visited the shores of Inis Cealtra, although I did discover a tale about this island which parallels one told of the man who may go down in history as one of Ireland's first exiles. It was Columcille, as he headed his boat towards Alba, who wrote:

From the plank of the oak where in sorrow I lie
I am straining my sight through the water and wind,
And large is the tear of the soft grey eye
Looking back on the land that it leaves behind.

One of the earliest Christians to be associated with Inis Cealtra was Colm of Terryglass, who died in the middle of the sixth century. But the man who is synonymous with the island is St. Caimin, half brother of the treacherous King of Connacht, Guaire. In the *Book of the Dun Cow* it is told that it was Guaire, in a colloquy with his half brother and St. Cummain, who chose the earth while the saints chose wisdom and pestilence respectively. In the *Book of Lismore* there is a story about Columcille which records that he too had such a discussion about the riches with which a church might best be endowed. St. Ciaran nominated that it might be filled with children; St. Cainnech opted for books of knowledge; St. Comgall asked that all the disease of the world might inhabit his own body; St. Columcille chose gold and silver.

The community on Inis Cealtra was raped by Turgesius but was re-established by Brian Boru. Brian's brother Marcan died here in 1010. The ruin known as St. Caimin's Church is attributed to Brian but the Romanesque doorway is twelfth century and it is known that some clumsy restoration work took place in the nineteenth century. The Romanesque doorway of St. Brigid's Church was also part of the restoration attempt.

Metal plaques have been erected by the Board of Works but most of these content themselves with warning the visitor, in Irish and English, of the fate that will befall them should they tamper with the stones. We are left to pick our way through the earthen mounds and the litter of fallen stones and to guess as best we can at their true meaning. As you walk through the Graveyard of the Saints, with the stone slabs of four centuries of the dead, and the Teampall bhFear nGonta, the Church of the Wounded Men, or stand at the round tower which may have been used as a sanctuary during raids, there is enough in the tranquillity of the place to satisfy the most inquisitive. We sat on a high mound on the island and took in the wonder of Lough Derg. It is not the best vantage point — for that

you must climb to the mountain heights which surround the lake –
but as the water moved through shades of blue and grey, as the
clouds scudded across the face of the sun, and as the swans of
Mountshannon whooped in across the bay after some distant
expedition, we would not have been surprised to have seen the
galleys of Brian Boru round the headland from Kincora.

The small town of Scarriff stands high above Lough Derg at the
head of Scarriff Bay, the westernmost extremity of the lake. To
reach the town we carefully skirted the Middle Ground and left
the bay for the meandering Scarriff River, which runs between cool
water meadows backed by light woodlands. An enormous white
ranch-type house stands on a small peninsula jutting into the lake
to the north of the steamer course and it is a much more useful
marker than the black and red stakes which are intended to show the
entrance to the river. The reed line here extends far out into the
lake and the beginning of the river passage is through this jungle of
green swords, which totally disguise the stakes until you are upon
them. The dredged channel is deep enough for most craft on the
lake but it twists and turns, narrowing all the time, and it is as well
to reduce speed to avoid an accident at some of the tree-shrouded
blind bends.

About a mile up the river we came to an old stone quay at which
a remarkable craft was moored. It consisted of a pontoon on which
a caravan shell had been mounted. The whole affair was topped
off with watertanks on the roof. No one seemed to be "at home"
so we passed the quay and soon reached a fork in the waterway in
the middle of which a sign directed us to Scarriff, and a few hundred
yards up the canal, which branches away from the river, we entered
the town harbour. The basin has been dredged, landscaped with
trees and grass and provided with a water supply. But in the midst
of all these endeavours no one seems to have thought of inserting a
few extra bollards. In the old Grand Canal Company days mooring
posts were placed at intervals of around sixty feet to accommodate
the barges. Try mooring a thirty-foot cruiser to these and you'd
need a lengthy gangplank to get ashore. We were forced to moor,
in rather unseamanlike fashion, to a somewhat insecure rubbish bin.

The town is only a few hundred yards from the harbour, along a rutted track which leads to the main road. As we crossed the bridge over the river we were astonished to discover that at this short distance from where we had turned into the cut, the water is a tumbling white water mountain torrent. The deep gorge of the river — Scarriff comes from Scairbh, a rugged, shallow ford — has been wrecked by a noisy and dirty chipboard factory, which straggles up the narrow valley in such a way that a mass of crude tin sheds and steaming pipes line the stream. From here the main street starts its climb to the market square which sits on a hill as though inviting the wind to do its worst. Because of the steepness of the place the backs of Scarriff houses are exposed to view and we were intrigued to discover that while the main street is a splendid splash of colour, with many of the houses and shops gaily painted, the view from the rear is of grey stone and cobbled yards. From that angle the whole place has the air of a north of England mining town.

But what Scarriff may lack in overall prettiness is more than made up for by the welcome on the mat of the shops and bars, and it is here that the Brian Merriman Tavern lies in a wynd off the main street.

> The Court considered the country's crisis,
> And what do you think its main advice is —
> That unless there's a spurt in procreation
> We can bid goodbye to the Irish nation;
> It's growing smaller year by year —
> And don't pretend that's not your affair.
> Between death and war and ruin and pillage
> The land is like a deserted village;
> Our best are banished, but you, you slob,
> Have you ever hammered a single job?
>
> What use are you to us, you cissy?
> We have thousands of women who'd keep you busy,
> With breasts like balloons or small as a bud,
> Buxom of body and hot in the blood,

Virgins or whores—whatever's your taste—
At least don't let them go to waste;
It's enough to make us broken hearted—
Legs galore—and none of them parted.
They're ready and willing for any endeavour—
But you can't expect them to wait forever.

So raged the "Hellish, hairy, haggard, hank, Bearded, bony, long and lank" ghoul of Brian Merriman's long poem, *The Midnight Court*, which has been given a boisterous and free translation by David Marcus. This eighteenth-century poem concerns a problem which has not yet been overcome, the unwillingness of Irishmen to get married while still in their prime. On previous visits the tavern had lived up to the riotous reputation of its namesake's verse, with many a fine band of minstrels taking the floor. At weekends the place comes alive. More the pity then that we arrived in the middle of the week.

What we lacked in company was made up for by a couple of stories we heard that night and since they might be of some interest to future Shannon navigators they had better be re-told. The first concerns the signpost which directs boatmen to leave the Scarriff River and enter the canal which leads to the harbour. When I happened to mention in the bar that evening that it seemed a very sensible bit of signposting, there was some astonishment that it should still be there, or at least that if it was there that I was safely moored in the harbour. It seems that a favourite pursuit of the young men of the town is to either remove the post or, and this is considered a far better game, to turn it in such a way that it points up the Scarriff River which, as I've said, turns quickly into a rocky torrent.

The other tale is a far more sophisticated bit of work. It is the habit of the local fishermen to leave their nets at the weekend and visit the town's drinking establishments in an attempt to encourage the tourists to hire their boats for a short cruise downriver and into the lake. By the time the boatmen have booked their clients the afternoon is well progressed and no one at all is fit to go sailing, but of course they do. One such boatload survived an erratic passage on the river only to emerge into the lake and immediately strike a rock. "Now, my man," said the visitor, "I thought you had assured us that you knew each and every rock in this lake." "Sure and I do," replied the boatman, "and this is the first one."

The distance from Carrick on Shannon to Killaloe is 110 miles, a few pleasant hours by car but more of a lifetime by water. In spite of our trips around the Shannon lakes by boat, and earlier by car, there were many hidden harbours we had failed to explore and one of these was to be our next port of call.

Dromineer lies some twelve miles from Scarriff, on the south-eastern shore of Dromineer Bay in County Tipperary. It is the headquarters of the Lough Derg Yacht Club, with the boathouse and slip hidden behind the shelter of Goose Island. The entrance to the bay, between Mountaineer Rock to the south and the Carrigeens to the north, is wide, and as we approached the shimmering water of a dead calm played tricks on our eyes. As we turned from the main channel round the black marker on Mountaineer a combination of heat haze and Bella Vista Point, a name which I didn't find in any Irish–English dictionary, hid the breakwater and I barely avoided piling *Fenniscourt* on to the rocks in the wrong bay. As we moved further east, however, we saw another cruiser emerging from the breakwater which marks the new harbour and set our course for her point of exit. We have often navigated the Shannon by such a means but on some occasion we are going to come unstuck and find that the boat on which we have taken a bearing has just extricated herself from some unfriendly rock.

The new harbour at Dromineer is among the largest on the Shannon and I am told that in summer it can resemble Cowes, with vast cruisers and tiny dinghies vying for the moorings. In one corner stands the old Grand Canal Company shed which once had an iron canopy extending across the water to protect the cargo while unloading. It is here that the greatest shelter is to be found, but a number of local boats are usually permanently moored here. Commanding the harbour is the ruin of a sixteenth-century castle which not only looks as though it is about to collapse but is fenced off in case someone should try to hasten the event.

Like many of the other harbours there is a pleasant promenade backed by grass lawns. A few modern bungalows are scattered round the edge. Add to this the Sail Inn, a guest house and village store, a telephone kiosk and a brief straggle of houses leading up the hill from the water and you have Dromineer. Setting out on a stroll we came upon a small bay with shallow dinghy landing stages and the only sandy beach we have ever seen on the Shannon. That was the extent of our stroll, and we must have looked a fine sight as we rolled up our trousers to take part in the curiously British pastime of paddling. The water, I might add, was like ice.

Dromineer lies in an exquisite lakeside setting with the wooded depths of Urra Point on the northern shore sheltering the stone-built mansion of Urra House with its greensward leading to a private harbour. But the village harbour has a number of drawbacks. Because of the wide bay the wind can hurl itself across the break-water and the basin is so large that the shoreside moorings can resemble a miniature hurricane. But the greatest curse of Dromineer is the dust, thanks to the limestone rim of the Shannon. This latter unpleasantness—and to say that when a car passes you must stand and wait until the dust storm settles is no exaggeration—persuaded us to give up our idea of walking inland. Instead, after lunch, we set out to row to the northern shore. After lazing around in the dinghy for an hour or two there was a bit of a wind rising. Being of a naturally lazy disposition I mounted the outboard on the transom and then discovered that the starting cord had been left on board *Fenniscourt*. It was a long row back.

Although the sun was still shining the wind continued to increase and it brought with it two boatloads of fishermen. Arriving at the harbour, they promptly set up their equipment on the breakwater and I could hardly believe my eyes when they began hauling in their lines with catch after catch. It was as though the wind had blown the fish into the harbour with them. I wandered over to the shop-cum-post-office-cum-boarding house where I was told that the fishermen were staying. They were on holiday from France and the scene before us was quite normal according to their landlady. She opened an enormous deep-freeze cabinet to reveal a good many hundredweight of gutted, frozen fish which, although not popular in Ireland, are considered excellent in France. Pike and perch made up the bulk of the catch, with a few trout.

The success of the French fishermen reminded me of a fine yarn I read in one of the first Shannon guides. A visitor was advised, should he feel the need for a salmon, to solicit the aid of the local water bailiff who would surely be able to find him a poached one. In fact there is a story of a fishing expedition which consisted of the local garda, the parish priest, the doctor and the local official to whom the salmon licence should have been paid. There can be little doubt that the Shannon, thanks to the lack of pollution, is a glorious fishing river and the parties of fishermen who hire boats there bear witness to the authenticity of the record-breaking claims.

The one that gets away on the Shannon is only likely to swim on to someone else's hook. Lough Derg is the earliest of the Mayfly lakes and the average trout weighs in at just under two pounds. There is a rather unfortunate story about a record trout catch near Mountshannon in 1861, when a fish weighing more than thirty pounds was landed. The poor fish was stuffed and stood proudly in the Irish National Museum. But museums are places where experts examine the wonders of the world and this wonder was later identified as a salmon. A thirty pound salmon is no wonder at all. But the strangest fishing adventure of them all took place near Portumna and it was Dom Kearns who provided the details. The story first appeared in *Rural Sports* in 1813. The author was a clergyman, but I am glad to say that for the benefit of his soul he had the gumption to point out that it had been told to him by a Major Bingham.

About seventeen years since, when visiting the late Marquis of Clanricarde at Portumna Castle, two Gentlemen brought to the Marquis an immense pike, which they had just caught in the River Shannon on the banks of which they had been taking their evening walk. Attracted by a noise and splashing of the water, they discovered in a little creek, a number of perch driven on shore and a fish which in their pursuit had so entangled himself with the ground as to have a great part of his body exposed and out of the water. They attacked him with an oar, that by accident lay on the bank, and killed him.

Never having seen any fish of this species so large, they judged it worth the observation of the Marquis, who equally surprised at its magnitude, had it weighed, and to our astonishment it exceeded the balance at ninety-two pounds; its length was such that when carried across the oar by the two Gentlemen who were neither of them short, the head and tail touched the ground. This may appear, and I own very much resembles a Munchausen, but Counsellor Doolan and Captain Henry Shewbridge are both alive, who took the monster and both reside at Portumna. Lord Clanricarde said it was the Genius of the Shannon and I termed it a second Python and recommended games to be annually celebrated in commemoration of the event.

Grace's bar at Dromineer is a fine and friendly establishment, but since Grace has been waiting for many years for a bar sign, and reckons that she will wait a good few more before the brewers provide it, there was a little delay while we searched for her house. Eventually we sited a number of casks and sure enough this grand temple to the *vin du pays* lay in front of us. The door was unbarred and we were soon sitting before a splendid carved bar, the richness of which was quite unusual for these parts. Below us, through a window in the gable of the house which framed the bay, lay *Fenniscourt Star*. Before us were drawn fine pints. The end of a perfect day.

TEN

In the Wake of St. Brendan

OUR COURSE LAY NORTHWARDS, back through Lough Derg, and it was not long before the low bridge at Portumna came into view. As the bridge-keeper had retired for the evening we moored to the wooden jetty which lies below the crossing. An overgrown cutting runs into the riverbank beside the new mooring place and this is where the canal barges used to shelter while waiting for the old hand-operated span to open.

We had arranged to meet our friends, the MacDonalds, and when they arrived we cast off and enjoyed a short cruise in the setting sun before returning to make our way for the last time to savour the glories of the Ferry Inn's kitchen. Had we visited this establishment many more times I would have been savouring the delights of the restaurant's kitchen sink. Later we adjourned to the bar to find our old friend, John Weaving, sitting with an empty jar. I filled it. He filled mine. And life was good. Later still Tony Lefroy called time and the party retired to *Fenniscourt Star* which seemed, in spite of a still night, to be doing a great deal of swaying. We broached a bottle of Paddy, just to steady the horizon, and the night was a long one. The hairs which John's dogs, Brocky and Twiggy, deposited throughout the saloon were only out-lengthened by the tales with which we entertained one another.

Later still the sun rose and I found myself lying on my bunk in the bow cabin without any idea of how I had got there. When we passed through the bridge and tied up at the fuel pumps, John

Lefroy wanted to know what we had been doing to John Weaving the previous evening since the poor man, while engaged on showing new hirers the ropes, had made several attempts to fall in the river.

It was time to head once more for Banagher where the MacDonalds had insisted that they return our hospitality. It was a sad journey. We were about to leave the river we had come to love and respect. We knew the ways of this waterway, the tricks and the pleasures. Ahead lay the unknown regions of the Grand Canal with, we were assured, all manner of hazards. If the Grand did not stop us then there was that farther river, the Barrow, and from tales I had heard of that place I had started to think that we required an amphibious tank rather than the fragile glass-fibre shell of *Fenniscourt Star*. But the unknown and the unexplored have a way of beckoning the traveller, and although we had read of the Barrow in the annals of other voyagers, we knew of no detailed log of this river which some had told us, in the same breath as they warned of rocks and rapids and unmarked weirs, rivalled all the rivers of Europe in the majesty of its course.

Arriving at the old harbour in Banagher we moored and I departed to telephone our friends. The lone telephone box was already inhabited but the good lady within was not holding the receiver to her ear. After ten minutes I knocked on the door and enquired if she was waiting for a call and she assured me that she was. It being the habit in Ireland for the telephone exchange to ring you back if you make a long distance call I thought no more of it, but after a further fifteen minutes I was growing restless. Now the great virtue of patience is nowhere better practised than in making a telephone call in the Republic of Ireland, but although I achieved some control of my city-bred haste it struck me that twenty-five minutes waiting time was excessive. Just as I was about to pursue the matter the occupant of the booth poked her head round the door and asked the time. It was one fifteen. It was then that I realised what was happening. Rather than waiting for the exchange to call she had arranged with someone to ring her at the call box at a specific time. What time, might I ask? Two o'clock, came the reply. Could I, perhaps, use the phone for a few minutes? Certainly you can, you should have asked before. As far as I could ascertain the reply was quite guileless. Time, in Banagher, had indeed stood still.

Lunch that day was a splendid coquilles de fruits de mer, washed down with an equally excellent German white. Ingrid and Malcolm MacDonald have only lived in Ireland for a few years but they have managed to locate the sources of the best gastronomic delights in a country where the riches of the earth and the sea are too often packed on to the first aircraft and delivered to the markets of London and Paris. Before anyone should accuse me of nationalistic proclivity, I should explain that Malcolm's lineage has long been removed from the heather hills of home. He was born in that well-known tartan town of Chipping Sodbury, thanks to the ardour of his great-grandfather, a doctor in Aberdeen who had the cheek to marry a Campbell. It is said that his patients found themselves another doctor overnight and the poor fellow was forced into exile.

Lunch complete, we all departed by car for Malcolm's favourite spot by Shannon banks and it was no time at all before he drew up at the diminutive Clonfert Cathedral, all that remains of a vast monastery. After a journey of more than one hundred and fifty miles by water, it was singularly inappropriate that we should arrive at this place by road rather than water. For this was the great Christian foundation established by St. Brendan the Navigator, the legends about whom, collected in *Navigatio Brendani*, were to have a considerable effect on medieval literature throughout the continent of Europe. It is said that the voyages of St. Brendan spurred on the adventurers of the Middle Ages to seek out India and the New World.

St. Brendan established his monastery at Clonfert, which is written in the *Book of Leinster* as Cluain-ferta, the meadow of the grave, in the middle of the sixth century, following his great voyage in search of the Promised Land. During his journey he made landfall on the Aran Islands and so, like his neighbour St. Ciaran of Clonmacnois, he too came under the influence of St. Enda and Ara's sun. The date and the fortunes of Clonfert closely parallel those of its neighbour, for, in spite of being out of sight of the Viking ships, Turgesius got wind of the settlement and stormed the buildings. The usual series of attacks followed until the monastery was completely wrecked in the sixteenth century. But the Protestants made some attempts at restoration in the seventeenth century and this continued, so that today Clonfert Cathedral, ascribed to a twelfth-century king, stands again in something approaching its original condition. It is still a place of worship for the Church of Ireland.

If Clonmacnois is a wonder of the Shannon for the vast complexity and division of its structures, then Clonfert is its equal for the delicacy of this gentle building set in a sheltered enclave of ancient walls and trees. To walk through the gates of the churchyard and stand before the Irish Romanesque doorway is a breathtaking experience. But although this doorway, with its chevron surrounding a great series of stone-carved grotesque human masks set in triangles and an arched colonnade, may be considered one of the finest examples of Romanesque architecture, the restorers have played their tricks on the original.

On looking closely we saw that during the rebuilding the workmen must have had a few spare carved heads about and these they simply stuffed into any available cranny. The richly-carved columns which surround the entrance lean inward, an architectural feature brought about by the need to reduce the length of the mighty single stone lintel which they would support. At Clonfert these jambs give way to a series of richly decorated arches and so the craftsman's carefully leaning stonework was not needed. This, however, simply provides a unique feature of the doorway and in no way detracts from its beauty. But a crudely embossed inner order was inserted for no apparent reason and the mason clearly did not consider following the line of his predecessor so that this, composed of sharply contrasting limestone, stands as straight as only the best plumb-line will allow. Sadly it spoils the effect of the doorway.

It is too easy in such a place to lay the blame for any offensive piece of stonework at the feet of some anonymous and long dead mason. The inner limestone order of the doorway was actually created in the fifteenth century. In the nineteenth century the newly appointed rector, the Reverend Robert McLarney, began an appeal to save the church and from his description of the building at the time there can be little doubt that without his enthusiasm what we see before us today would be no more than a roofless ruin:

> The cathedral was literally the abode of the rat, the bat and the beetle. Noisome insects crawled all over the place. The walls were covered with ugly modern plaster and were reeking with damp, the atmosphere of the cathedral resembled that of a charnel house. The floor was greatly decayed. Small trees and shrubs grew on the roof which leaked badly.

The interior of Clonfert Cathedral contains little of interest but as we stood beside the choir stalls we discovered a curious effigy, seemingly carved out of the solid stone. It was a mermaid, holding the traditional comb and mirror, naked from the waist up, her bosoms polished smooth, while the stone of the chancel arch remained dull and lustreless. This, announced Malcolm, was a relic of considerable archaeological, historical and sociological importance and his researches had shown that the glowing radiance of the young lady's contours were the result of centuries of choir boys brushing past to their seats. He could not account for the sculpting of this unclerical figure before the altar but the Dean of Clonfert, the Very Reverend Cyril Champ, had two interesting theories as to how this fifteenth-century figure came to be placed in the cathedral. He reminded us of the belief that St. Brendan reached the shores of North America where he possibly saw many seals. One particular branch of the seal family, called dugong, has a head similar in shape to that of a human and so arose the idea of mermaids. The Dean also thought that there might be some connection between the legend that St. Brendan preached to the fishes from the back of a whale. In fact he sent us a Christmas card printed by the Iona Community which pictured the saint engaged in this unlikely service. The drawing, by J. H. Miller, shows Brendan's boat moored to the whale and the good saint standing beside a fire which the whale had invited his guest to light on his back.

The flower of Clonfert is not the cathedral however, but something which, though planted by man, was finished with elaborate

Commercial days: loading Guinness at the Dublin canal terminus for the run to Limerick.

The Grand Canal Mecca. A converted and much decorated horse-drawn barge heads out of Robertstown. In the background is the renovated canal hotel.

Sean Fitzsimon's boat, *Ye Iron Lung*.

Mike Thomas at the tiller of *Celtic Lady*, the first English canal narrow boat to navigate the Grand Canal.

care by nature. Malcolm took us over a low wall and into the light woodland which surrounds the building. After a few minutes scrambling through the undergrowth he told us to close our eyes and led us a little further forward. When we opened our eyes it was to see something of such tranquil beauty that it will be gently etched on our memories for many years to come. Before us lay a carpet of velvet moss lined on both sides by yews of great age. The sun cast shards of silver light between the drooping, gnarled branches which formed the spandril of the arch and where these touched the moss it turned to the colour of copper. The leaves, caught in the light, were a hundred shades of green. This was nature's cloister, perhaps, or the true cathedral of Clonfert. Whoever planted this walk had an elaborate plan in mind, for the main avenue, running from east to west, is joined by two shorter avenues running from north to south, thus forming the transept of a leafy church. At the end of this enchanted glade we came out before the Bishop's Palace which, though marked along with the cathedral on the Ordnance Survey map, seemed a motley heap of no architectural interest. However the last occupant of the house, Sir Oswald Mosley, who lived there in the early 1950s, found the place "rambling and romantic rather than beautiful".

The ancient cathedral at Clonfert, with its tree-formed reflection, made a fitting end to our exploration of Shannonside and it seemed appropriate that the holy place of another earlier navigator should have provided us with the most exquisite memory of the voyage. If St. Brendan visited the Isle of Paradise on his voyage, as legend tells us, we would like to think that he transferred some of the radiant glories of that place to his college by the Shannon. For it is a place which merits equally the adjectival outpourings of the scribe who described "a land odorous, flower-smooth, blessed, a land many-melodied, musical, shouting for joy, unmournful".

Brendan Daly claims no descent from his saintly namesake, and he is certainly not known for saying Mass while perched on the back of a whale. His Promised Land extends no further than a watery line from Dublin to Shannon Harbour, the Grand Canal, and from Lowtown to St. Mullins, the Barrow line of the canal and the River

Barrow itself. If a new edition of the *Navigatio Brendani* should be produced, however, the modern miracles of Brendan Daly might well provide an appendix, and his navigational annals may be consulted at the headquarters of Córas Iompair Eireann, the Irish state transport authority, which has ordained this gentleman, as their Special Projects Engineer, to minister over the ancient creaks, cracks, leaks, racks, subsidences, breaches and general hazards to navigation of the waterways under their control. Brendan is assisted in this crusade by John McNamara — called Mr. Mac to his face and Big Mac to his back—who is based at the canal maintenance depot at Tullamore, a town noted for an expensive whiskey liqueur, the worst fish and chip shop in Ireland, and a canal harbour, the entrance to which has a kink in it designed to give the boat-proud a heart attack.

Brendan's predecessors, the directors of the Grand Canal Company, made an annual sortie along the canal to ascertain that their channel, unlike some others, did hold water. The trip was a merry event and at one of the board meetings held during its progress, the voyagers resolved to dispense with the rule limiting the consumption of wine to one pint per man. The habit, the annual cruise that is, not the wine bibbing, continues and since the CIE inspection coincided with part of our own journey along the canal we had arranged to meet Brendan and John at Banagher.

Our gallivanting around the countryside that day meant that stocks of food were low and we gladly accepted their invitation to dine on board *Boyle Star*, another cruiser in the Emerald Star fleet. Our pleasure increased when Brendan emerged from the tiny galley with four plates of fillet steak. His wife Peggy, who joined us later in the voyage, was at pains to explain that this was all Brendan was capable of cooking. It seemed to be a dreadful inconvenience, a bit like those who can only stomach champagne. After dinner we set out to paint the town red but, to coin a phrase used by someone about Tarmonbarry, due to the "inconsiderableness" of the place we only managed a feeble pink.

Next morning even the birds of Banagher were aroused by the departure of some ardent boatman and lurching bleary-eyed from my foam-cushioned hammock I was just in time to see the stern of

Boyle Star vanish upstream. I resolved to read a moral lesson to her crew about Irishmen who tell foreigners about how long it takes people to adjust to the rhythm of native life and put the kettle on for breakfast.

Part II

There's manys a man on the Grand Canal
Who'd face both a judge and jury
If only his craft would swing abaft
And finish in Guinness's brewery.

ELEVEN

The Grand Canal

LET THEM EAT BOG. They did just that in 1935 when Robert Lloyd Praeger and a group of eminent botanists met in the midst of a watered desert. They came from Oxford and Cambridge, Stockholm and Copenhagen, and the wet wind soughed round a great onomatopaeic discussion on the precise interpretation of words like soligenous, topogenous and ombrogenous. They sank almost to their knees as the bog, unused to such a weight of wisdom, was unable to support them and the chatter only ceased when two of their number, "in an endeavour to solve the question of the origin of the peat, would chew some of the mud brought up by the boring tool, to test the presence or absence of gritty material in the vegetable mass".

A bog and a canal have only one thing in common: a presence of water. While the one sucks and spews, heaves and bursts, the other demands a strong stable bank and bed. Building a canal through a bog is a little like stopping a belly dancer in mid-gyration. This was the biggest headache which the canal engineers had to face. As the bog was flat the pounds, or levels as the stretches between locks are known in Ireland, were very long. As the bog sank ever greater embankments were required to contain the water channel. When these were weakened by movement of the substructure the pressure of millions of gallons of water threatened to burst the banks. No fewer than four breaches have occurred in the great embankment west of the Blundell Aqueduct, thirty-eight miles from Dublin, on a level of more than eighteen miles. The most recent of these, in 1975, took place near Daingean.

On our first brief visit to the Grand Canal some years ago, when we locked into the canal basin at Shannon Harbour for an overnight stop on our way down the Shannon, the only leak that Val and I could discover was coming from above rather than below. The wind and rain intensified as we sat down to supper and nature made a farce of a still water canal as our craft was buffeted against the stone quay. As the storm reached its pitch the thunder bawled out from the furious clouds and great shards of white lightning silhouetted the windowless ruin of the Grand Canal Company's hotel outside our cabin window. It was a night for a good book by the fireside, but in a constantly bucking boat there was little pleasure to be had, although we were thankful to be dry and warm. In a fit of reckless abandon, brought on by a rapidly dwindling supply of Paddy, we donned oilskins and stout boots and slipped and slithered our way along the quay to the nearest hostelry.

The scene that night resembled some dramatic reincarnation of Tam o' Shanter with the roofless hotel, the tangled interior "in a bleeze", taking the place of Kirk Alloway. Perhaps it was Auld Nick's night off the pipes for there was certainly not "a winsome wench and walie" in sight and the citizens of Shannon Harbour were more inclined to the wearing of gumboots and sou'westers than cutty sarks of "whatever harn". It must have been in weather such as this that Charles Lever saw the place in *Jack Hinton, The Guardsman*.

A prospect more bleak, more barren, it would be impossible to conceive – a wide river with low reedy banks, moving sluggishly on its yellow current between broad tracts of bog or callow water meadow land; no trace of cultivation, not even a tree to be seen. Such is Shannon Harbour.

No one ever had a kind word for this place. Trollope in *The Kellys and the O'Kellys* was full of nauseating details of the "collops of the raw animal and vast heaps of yellow turnip" served to travellers on the passage boats making their way along the canal. As early as 1819 James Dawson, in a series of letters to the *Carrick Morning Post*, later published as a pamphlet on canal extensions, was writing of this tiny canalside settlement.

It is the great misfortune of the main trunk of the Grand Canal that it passes through districts for the most part boggy and barren, and the traders and passengers would be dreadfully disappointed upon finding themselves at the termination of the Grand Canal, in the wretched village of Shannon Harbour, without decent accommodation or entertainment of any kind.

With Lever and Dawson raging about the village and the land-scape, and Trollope adding his literary weight on the subject of the food, it is hardly surprising that the modern navigator may give pause for thought before making a passage along the cut. I was reminded, however, of a pleasant month's cruising in England which had included the Staffordshire and Worcester Canal, that "stinking ditch" which the inhabitants of Bewdley on the Severn would not have enter the river through their township. Stinking it was not, and delightful was the trip. Such is also true of the Grand and the much maligned village of Shannon Harbour, for once inside the hard-pewed grocery-cum-bar we were ensconced in a world of muffled talk and mulled stout where the extremes outside only emphasised the luxury of chance meeting inside a village bar. Our conversation, about the weather, of course, was only interrupted by the butting forth of the door as the swirling gale made to enter on the heels of yet another villager drawn towards our com-munion by the loneliness such howling weather can provoke.

Our second entry into the Grand Canal was undertaken beneath brighter skies and at a more humane hour than that chosen by Brendan and John. As we passed into the narrow channel, with Bullock Island to the south and a nameless island to the north, we could see the silt bank thrown up across our passage by the River Brosna. But by keeping well to the south bank, where a new wood and scaffold staging, built by John Weaving, provides a handy landing place for crews wishing to operate the lock, we were able to make our way towards the first canal lock of our voyage. The locks

are numbered from Dublin, so this was thirty-sixth lock. We just
caught the glimpse of a boat in the chamber as the gates swung shut
but no amount of waving and shouting had any effect.

The waterways of Britain are surrounded by a quixotic number of
rules and regulations, some dating from the days of the ark, some
from Big Brother, the British Waterways Board, and others simply
gentlemen's agreements designed to ease a journey. There is the
matter of "your water". A boat waiting below a full lock, on seeing
another boat approaching downhill, should wait until the other
craft has entered the full lock and locked down. By so doing a lockful
of water is saved and the boat crew waiting to pass uphill will have
been saved the effort of emptying the chamber as well as filling it.
Today, when a great many canal craft do not fully occupy a lock, it
is equally courteous to wait on any following craft to see if both may
pass through together. Two crews make half the work.

Climbing up to the lock and seeing that there was room for a ship
of the line astern of its occupant I asked if the crew would wait at
the thirty-fifth lock, only 220 yards away, until we had passed
through and could join them. This way we would have avoided a
hard passage with every lock set against us. But they were in a hurry
to reach Tullamore by nightfall and did not seem at all keen on the
idea. Many years of canal travel have made me sanguine about
haste. Most canals were designed to take horsedrawn traffic which
caused much less turbulence than motor-driven craft. In the long
term speedhogs simply undercut the banks and hasten a breach,
apart from sending your dinner on to your lap if you happen to be
moored when they pass. More immediately, and something which
might give crews more cause to slow down since it is their own
pleasure which is going to be affected, the draught of a boat in-
creases with its speed and the faster you go the more likely it is
that your prop will pick up a plastic bag or some other obstacle
dumped by a thoughtless landsman. My thoughts on the subject
must have been prophetic for when we reached Lowtown we heard
that our hasty crew had to be craned from the water with forty feet
of barbed wire round their prop. As Michael Walsh, a Dublin travel
agent and frequent inland navigator wrote some years ago after
picking up a mattress: "Every canal has a bed but apparently the

Grand Canal is more fully equipped." On that occasion the Crumlin Fire Brigade rose to the rescue with wire cutters.

As Speedy Gonzales and his crew left the lock I closed the top gates behind them, emptied the lock, opened the lower gates, and Val cruised into the chamber. That was when the trouble started. Brendan and John had asked us not to be put off the canal by the condition of the first two locks which were about to have new gates installed. What they didn't tell us was that you would have needed to harness a bull to the beams to close the bottom gates. Val climbed on to the lockside but even our combined effort could not move the gates. One of the great attractions of the Grand Canal is that the locks are manned, although the rundown in traffic means that one man may operate as many as four locks. Little did we know that in the moment of our greatest need the lock-keeper was up the line, talking with Brendan and John. I was just about to break every canal law in the book and open a top rack to see if the flow of water would help close the gate when another craft came slowly up the channel from the Shannon.

On deck stood one of the most enormous men we had ever seen and, since his height was matched by his weight, his every movement sent his tiny cruiser slewing from side to side. Our rescuers turned out to be two Germans who had spent six happy summers cruising the Shannon. This information took some time to impart since the giant's English was about as good as my German which is non-existent. They were, he announced, very glad to see us since his friend had only one leg and was unable to jump on and off the boat. Judging by the stacked crates of Guinness in the open cockpit, Val suggested that it was unlikely he would ever have any need to get off the boat again. This prompted a great deal of laughing and backslapping which almost resulted in my falling, or was I being pushed, into the drink? Now, announced our new friend, they were going to try their hand at the Grand Canal. With which I suggested that he might as well do just that and close the bottom gates. He did.

Jim Feaney's wife was waiting to help us through the next lock and before we had filled it Jim himself appeared. I explained our problem at the first lock and Jim's concern and consideration for our plight was only slightly spoiled by his crack that "that, of course, is why you'll never find me there". He soon had us through and while we set off on the trip of just over a mile to thirty-fourth lock Jim motored along the line to have it ready for our arrival. The same process was repeated for thirty-third lock.

Lock thirty-three is a double lock, the equivalent of an English staircase and not, as the name suggests, a set of parallel locks like the trio at Hillmorton on the northern section of the Oxford Canal where the British Waterways Board have their workshop and hire base. None of the Irish staircases is of more than two steps but what they may lack in height—the staircase on the Grand Union Canal at Foxton consists of two rises of five steps—they make up for in awkwardness. Bridges were built at many of the locks on the Grand Canal and Val and I are convinced that the builders held some grudge against the men who would sail through the cut. At Belmont double lock the bridge-builder achieved the ultimate in impracticability.

As we approached the lower chamber we could see a bridge crossing it at the top end and covering a good third of the lock. We moored to a row of old warehouses on the left bank and made our way up to where Jim was preparing the locks. To our left, by the road which crosses the bridge, we could see the River Brosna which runs parallel to the canal for some fifteen miles. With the lock empty I returned to *Fenniscourt Star* and took her into the chamber. With the other boat astern I had to nudge the bows right up to the bottom gate and that was when I started to curse the bridge and its builder. It was impossible to get a bow rope ashore from beneath the bridge. With the bottom gates closed Jim lifted the racks and all hell was let loose as *Fenniscourt Star* pounded from side to side in the lock. When water decides to have its way there is nothing that can be done to stop it. The water from the upper chamber shot across the cill and straight over our bows and forecabin. I was quite pleased at this instant form of scrub down until I noticed water pouring under the door to the forecabin. Opening it I found that the water pressure was so great that it had found a way round the edges of the tightly fastened windows. There was nothing for it but to switch on the bilge pump and make ready for a grand mopping-up ceremony later in the day.

As with our problems at thirty-sixth lock Jim had a word to say about the latest fiasco for had he not been told only to let one boat through Belmont at a time so that it might lie back against the lower gates and thus avoid the torrent? It was quite beyond me to understand why he had not followed this procedure. Once through we tied to the bank, waved goodbye to the German crew, and set about wringing out those clothes stowed beneath the bunks which had received the full effect of Jim Feaney's attentions at the breast racks. Having completed the mopping up we vowed to lock ourselves through future locks, or at least to take careful command of any enthusiastic keeper.

In 1765 a canal was begun to be cut from Dublin and intended to be continued to Athlone, which is about seventy English miles off, in order to open a communication with the Shannon; at the rate the work is at present carried on it bids fair for being completed in three or four centuries.

Richard Twiss was a member of an exclusive fraternity of eighteenth-century travellers who, thanks often to vast family inheritances, were not only able to move freely through Europe but to publish their observations. Twiss covered 27,000 miles through Holland, Belgium, France, Switzerland, Italy, Germany, Bohemia, Portugal and Spain before he arrived in Ireland in 1775. His *Tour in Ireland* was published the following year. The comments were not altogether facetious. The subject of a canal to link Dublin with the Shannon and Barrow was first mooted in an Act of Parliament passed in the reign of George I in 1715 but, in spite of a further Act in 1721, the southern waterway system was shelved. James Brindley, thought by many to be the father of the British canal, was a stripling of fifteen when work began on the Newry Canal in the north in 1731. Twenty years later the grandly titled Corporation for Promoting and Carrying on an Inland Navigation in Ireland had been established but their promotions were negligible and by 1770 they had been replaced by the equally grandly titled Company of the Undertakers of the Grand Canal.

The first engineer was Thomas Omer who surveyed a line as far

as Sallins, about twenty miles from Dublin. There followed a great
number of engineers who dabbled in the construction with varying
degrees of success and I would dearly like to know how the right
honourable and honourable gentlemen of the navigation board
received the news that in some places their noble canal was four and
five feet deeper than at others. This is a little like building a tunnel
from both ends and failing to meet in the middle. One can only be
thankful that there was no need for tunnels in Ireland; there are
quite enough, complete with their kinks, in England. In 1773, John
Smeaton, engineer of the Forth and Clyde Canal, arrived to survey
the line. His assistant, William Jessop, later to become known as a
canal and railway engineer in England, took part in a number of
advisory surveys but the bogs, which Smeaton had advised against
crossing, the short cuts taken by contractors, and the temptation to
the navvies of better work across the sea, were a continual hindrance.

By 1803 the connection with the Shannon was almost complete,
the last lock opening on to the confluence of the River Brosna with
the larger river. The meeting point was a bad one since the Brosna
kept throwing up a silt bar across the exit. The same thing had
occurred at the Dublin end where the River Dodder formed a bar
across the entrance to the Grand Canal Docks. But the Court of
Directors would not be stifled in their moment of glory. They had
reached the Liffey in 1796, made contact with the Barrow at Athy
in 1791, and happy days and splendid profits lay ahead. Although
today we may think of the canal as an entity, the process of building
in four distinct sections with various branches gave rise to the term
of the Main Line, running for twenty-six miles from James's Street
Harbour to Lowtown, the Barrow Line, running for twenty-eight
miles from Lowtown to Athy, Shannon Line running for fifty-three
miles from Lowtown to Shannon Harbour, and the Circular Line
passing through Dublin to the Liffey for four miles.

Passage through canals is generally a fairly grubby proceeding, but
a grand nautical affair, complete with flotillas, flagships and bands,
was planned for the Shannon breakthrough. The Directors set
down their ideas with a flourish in the Minutes of September 1803:

Ordered that the Inspector of Passage Boats do serve notice on the different Contractors for drawing the Company's Passage Boats that they are to prepare eight additional horses at each stage from Dublin to Tullamore, to draw the four extra Passage Boats intended to leave Dublin on Sunday morning the ninth of October next at six o'clock to convey the Undertakers to Tullamore that day, and to apprize them that they are to draw these Boats in the same time as the Boats now in commission, or be subject to the like fines, and also to inform them to be prepared to draw the same Boats back from Tullamore on Tuesday morning to set off at six o'clock, the like time to be kept as in drawing the Passage Boats; the difference of time of setting off from Dublin and Tullamore respectively to be added or deducted from the rated time published (of which he is to give due notice) by which they can ascertain the correct time of arrival at each stage.

The Directors will furnish the first four drivers with the use each of one outside coat, one jacket, one pair of trousers, one gold-laced hat for the boat that leads the van, and one silver-laced hat to each of the other three.

N.B. They are to have good boots or shoes, clean stockings and shirt etc. and drive horsemanlike; all the above coats, jackets, trousers and hats, they are to exchange with the Drivers at the Stages they arrive at instantaneously to be deprived of the perquisite to be given by the Board for their activity and sobriety; the same mode to be observed on the return from Shannon Harbour.

The Board also desire that Mr. Spray shall procure two additional Boat Masters for the trip in addition to the two Supernumerary Ones (Fanel the Commander of the Suck Cattle Boat may be one of them) also four neat Boat Mistresses and Maids, four Mates and four Steerers, these boats the Masters are to furnish with every accommodation such as Tea equipage, glasses, plates, knives etc. to provide a breakfast and a cold collation each day, and its appurtenances, to be paid for at the time by the passengers, in the manner and at the same rates as in the Passage Boats. Mr. Spray is to procure from Mr. Ross eight grapple irons with cords attached, two for each boat, and to be coiled and placed in the most convenient place, so as to take up any person

falling overboard, and not accustomed to long voyages. Each boat
is to be furnished with two mooring chains and two iron pins, lest
there should not be posts at proper places for all the boats . . .

The order of movement. The *Hardwicke* to lead the van, with
the Grand Junction Emblematic Standard erected, and the Band
of Music on board to play "God Save the King" at every town.
2. The *Lea* with her colours. 3. The *Huband* next. 4. The *Latouche*
in the rere. To follow each other immediately through each lock.

The Board deem it absolutely necessary that Mr. Spray should
have his horse to attend the Grand Junction Flotilla to convey
such orders as may be requisite to be issued from the Flag Ship
or for any other purpose. Query? Are the arms necessary to be
put aboard the Boats.

Ordered that Captain Evans do use every means in his power
to have the Levels of the whole line up; and the lock-keepers and
their families to be dressed in their best apparel, the places neat
and lock houses white-washed, and he is to order each Boat's
crew to give three cheers as the Royal Grand Canal Standard
passes them: all Boats, passage boats and others to and from
Dublin to give way to the Grand Junction Flotilla.

The only thing to give way in the autumn of 1803 was the bank
of the Grand Canal and it was not until 1805 that the bog levels
were made staunch and regular services could proceed along the
Shannon Line. The work had taken half a century to complete but
although canals in England were to be soon overshadowed by that
new miracle transport system, the railway, the Grand Canal of
Ireland survived as a profitable entity for many years, much to the
astonishment of its earlier critics. There was an attitude prevalent
at the time that much of the engineering work being carried on was
simply an attempt to relieve poverty. Thus that earliest canal
enthusiast and historian, John Phillips, in his *General History of
Inland Navigation, Foreign and Domestic*, may quote one observer,
describing the canal: "It's a job, it was meant as a job; you are not
to consider it as a canal of trade, but as a canal for public money."

Phillips had read Arthur Young's 1780 *Tour in Ireland* and he
extracted from it in his chapter on the "Canal from the City of

The amazingly complicated bascule bridge at Monasterevan on the Barrow Line of the Grand.

The Barrow in 1937. Manually operated capstans like this were used to haul boats against the flow of the river.

Carlow has one of the few marked weirs on the Barrow, which is just as well, since the boat stream passes under the town bridge and then sweeps across the river from east to west immediately above the white water.

Not some ancient fortress, but castellated maltings below Milford weir. The boat stream leading to the canal and lock runs perilously close to the weir and boats must hug the west bank to avoid being caught in the current.

Dublin to the River Shannon". Among the conclusions drawn was that "if this Grand Canal was entirely completed, the navigation of it, including whatever the country towns took from Dublin, would prove of such little account, that it would remain a greater monument of folly, if possible, than at present". On the contrary. When the Grand Canal Company was nationalised in 1950, and the operation of the canal and the company's boats absorbed into Córas Iompair Eireann, the last Chairman of the company emphasised that they were neither bankrupt nor had asked for Government assistance. In 1939 the company's barges carried a total of 120,025 tons. In 1949 it was 111,462 tons and, after nationalisation, the figure for 1956 was 89,640 tons. The last figure includes a massive 26,020 tons of porter and it was the carriage of Guinness which did much to sustain the canal before the withdrawal of commercial trading in January 1960.

Ironically, when Guinness was no longer shipped from Dublin to Limerick by canal, vast storage sheds had to be built at the delivery point since the rail depot could not cope with the additional tonnage. It is necessary for Guinness to settle in the cask for some time before delivery to your glass. The placid four-day journey by canal allowed for this period but the brief train journey did not. That, said one old Guinness hand, is what they call progress.

Dry and liquid cargoes were not the only items to be carried on the canal. As in England there was a regular passenger boat service and in order to provide greater comfort for their passengers the Grand Canal Company established a series of canal-side hotels. These are unique to Ireland. They were all of vast four-square proportions and it is staggering to observe, as you approach a tiny village like Robertstown, which mainly consists of low single-storey structures, the great bulk of the hotel rising above the canal. The earliest account of passage-boat travel on the Irish canals was revealed by N. W. English in an article on Waterway Travellers published in *Canaliana*, the magazine of the Robertstown Muintir na Tire. It comes from the venerable diaries of the founder of Methodism, the Rev. John Wesley:

Wednesday 22nd June, 1785. I went with twelve or fourteen of our friends, on the Canal to Prosperous. It is a most elegant way of travelling, little inferior to that of Trackskuyts in Holland. We had fifty or sixty persons in the boat, many of whom desired me to give them a sermon. I did so and they were all attention. After preaching at five in the morning Thursday 23rd, I took boat with a larger company than before, who about eleven desired me to preach.

None of the Grand Canal's passage boats have been preserved but a number of the old cargo vessels were bought privately and converted into comfortable cruising homes. Sadly, however, the Shannon traveller is more likely to catch a glimpse of them than those who decide to cruise the canal. This is partly due to the shallower depth of the canal since commercial traffic ceased, but it is also true that the Shannon provides the boatman with few of the rigours of the canal.

To get some idea of the peace and tranquillity of the Irish water-ways it is only necessary to examine Borde Fáilte figures for hire craft. At the last count there were 287 craft, only four of these being permanently based on the 190 miles of the canal. For some years now Emerald Star Line, whose interest in the inland waterways has a campaigning zeal not usually associated with a commercial company, has set up a temporary springtime base on the River Barrow, thus increasing the hire fleet to around a dozen craft. Britain's inland mariners, with their memories of high summer lock jams, line abreast moorings and tank-driver captains bent on wiping out anyone who gets in their way, will readily appreciate the benefits of the Irish system.

Five locks into the Grand Canal and our legs and arms were already aching but we knew that a ten-mile level pound lay before us, followed by only two locks before we would reach our overnight mooring at Rahan, where Brendan and John would be. Although we were still running parallel to the River Brosna any impression of passing through a valley was soon dispelled as we entered the first bogland of our canal passage. Bleak, desolate and wild would have been our journey had it not been for the gigantic walls of vivid yellow furze lining the banks and stretching out across the bog. The cooling towers of Ferbane Power Station, with a capacity of eighty megawatts, the largest peat-fired station in Ireland, broke the flat horizon to the south although the town of that name lies a good mile to the north of the canal. A glance at the Ordnance Survey map confirmed that we were pressing further and further into a no man's land of swamp.

By now heavy rain clouds were assembling from the west and a sharp chill breeze sent tiny waves scudding across the surface of the water. The sun sliced through the thin gaps between the clouds and sent a ghostly silver light waving like a curtain across the forbidding country, making the furze dance luminously along the banks and laying magic shades across the rising mass of the Slieve Blooms ten miles away. We had intended stopping here and there along the bank but the approach of the storm persuaded us to remain in the comfort of *Fenniscourt*'s cabin. Shortly after crossing the Macartney Aqueduct over the delightfully named but rather brackish Silver River, we came to Derry Bridge where a bad breach in 1954 closed the canal for four months. A few houses appeared along the line as we approached the village of Pollagh, the name meaning a place full of holes or pits being an apt reminder of the dangers in the surrounding bog. Many of the houses had a tree outside strung with brightly coloured ribbons and bunches of cut flowers. Children came tumbling from the thatched cottages to wave us on our way, farm dogs yapping at their heels. The access road to many of these houses is by way of the towpath, which provides the only solid route across the bog and this has given rise to maintenance problems since, although designed to take the wear and tear of horse-drawn vehicles, the banks cannot sustain the weight of modern farm machinery.

The area around Pollagh and the further bog village of Rahan has found a new prosperity with the establishment of a power station and peat workings but it is an isolated part of the midlands where old customs are still retained. We were now in the first days of May and the gaily-decorated trees were in celebration of May Day. Not the Socialist festival but that of Bealtaine. In Scotland the word is Beltaine, a Gaelic word meaning literally "the blaze kindling". It was the custom of the Druids to light two fires at this time and drive cattle between them, believing that by so doing their stock would be protected. The theory is known as sympathetic magic; by performing certain rituals paralleling those of nature, the Gods would look kindly on the celebrants.

Many such events were later converted to abide by Christian doctrine and the fire ceremony of Bealtaine was transferred to Midsummer's Eve. An event making use of cattle but avoiding sacrifice by simply burning bones in the fires has been carried out in Ireland, but I was unable to discover whether this is still held. In Cornwall, however, a ceremony is still performed each year by the Old Cornwall Societies. We attended one of these events high on the moors above Wadebridge on the eve of St. John when bonfires made a circle of flame around the coast at midnight. The veil of Christian respectability only thinly disguised the pagan ritual as the celebrant prepared to throw her wild flowers, no doubt easier to find than bones, on the fire. And so the Sun God was invoked to give blessing to the land.

The first smattering of rain arrived when we reached thirty-first lock and so we passed through and continued on to thirtieth lock where we decided to wait out the storm and, if needs be, spend the night there. But we reckoned without the curious behaviour of an Irish lock-keeper.

Walter Mitchell is one of the Grand Old Men of the Grand Canal. Brendan and John had recommended his company to us and him to ours as they passed by and as we moored Walter came down from his house to introduce himself and invite us inside for a cup of tea.

"But first," announced Walter, "we'll be getting you through the lock."

"Perhaps," I suggested, "we should wait for the storm to pass and after a few cups of tea the sun may be out."

"No man knows what may happen after a few cups of tea," came the reply.

With that Walter disappeared back to the lock and the next thing we saw were the gates opening through the arch of the bridge. Naturally the storm chose that moment to give full vent to its feelings but Walter seemed quite unmoved by the fact that there was as much water falling from the heavens as passing through his precious racks. It took a long time and Walter took even longer to get through the chamber at Rahan. And at the end of it all, what do you think the man said?

"But sure now and we all feel like a cup of tea."

A curious logic, but a logic none the less.

Walter's house is small and comfortable and, although like many lock houses built on the canal embankment, the one-storey structure you see from the canal turns out to be two storeys on the landward side, I still suspect the place of having elastic walls since Walter and his wife reared no fewer than twelve children in the place. The "tea" came out of small metal containers labelled Harp and Guinness and Mrs. Mitchell was soon thrusting great piles of chicken sandwiches upon us from the taste of which we could tell that no bland broiler ever darkened the door. As the wind and the rain worked themselves into a fury outside, Walter fumbled in cupboards and after each sortie would emerge with another cluster of "teas". He caught sight of me glancing at the mantelshelf.

"Now don't go worrying yourself about that," he said. "A friend brought that to the house."

I had no idea what it was that I was not to worry about but for the next few minutes I was scanning the area for some dreadful token. Eventually I decided that a single Easter lily was the cause of Walter's concern. It was a memory of the Easter Rising fifty years before.

Walter comes from a long line of canal families, the longest line since he can boast that a Mitchell has been connected with the waterway since its inception and that the records show an overseer named Mitchell employed during the construction. The family is Scottish, Protestant and Republican which is as many apparently irreconcilable antecedents as you are likely to find in Ireland. Walter worked in his cousin's drapery in Tullamore when he was a lad but in the early thirties he came back to live in his father's lock house and eventually took over. He cannot remember the precise date he started but he's been more than forty years at Rahan lock and depot and, now seventy-five, looks as though he'll be there for another forty. He has a bit of a limp since a few years ago he was cycling along the towpath in a misty dawn and had an unfortunate collision with a cow. Walter went head-first over the startled beast which lashed out in alarm. Apart from this he has no complaints. He had a wealth of information to impart and it is best that he tells his story himself.

"In the old days Rahan was a staging post where horses were changed. You can still see the remains of the stables and the out-houses where the horse drivers could rest overnight. But sometimes it was a bit hard to tell night from day for when the Guinness boats were working twenty-four-hour shifts they would arrive here at two-thirty or three-thirty a.m. and I'd have to be out of bed and working them through. There wasn't a light to be seen. The boat-men didn't like lights on the boats as they found it easier to adjust to the gloom, than be blinded by another craft approaching with a searchlight on the bows. There's a nice one I heard somewhere about one of us keepers who was asked by a gent from Dublin how many years he had worked for the company. Your man said a hun-dred years and when the Dublin man asked how he arrived at the figure he got told that it reckoned out at fifty years by day and fifty years by night. Mind you at that time the pay was pitiful and the country lock-keepers were paid even less than those in the towns. By God, we were the poorest of the poor. So most of us had another job here and there. I did a bit of farming and I still keep a few cows on a parcel of land since I like to have my own milk and none of that bottled stuff.

"There have been some queer events at Rahan. We were always having inspectors and engineers arriving to look for possible damage and, of course, they'd always know better than any Tom, Dick or Walter of a lock-keeper. I remember that the dredger arrived just below the lock and though I warned the boys that they were cutting too deep, they would have nothing of it. Next morning there was a bloody great lake in a hollow a few hundred yards from the canal and not enough to wash your big toe with along the line. But the tale I like best is of the famous local well which everyone swore by. It came out near a spot where the farmer swam his cattle from bank to bank. You'll know just what happened. Along came CIE to repair the trampled banks and lay a concrete underwater channel down the sides of the embankment to halt the erosion. Next day the damned well was dry. And that was the end of Rahan's legendary spring, not that everyone cares to remember the legend."

Time was when no farmer would have allowed his animals to stray along the line for the old Canal Company offered a reward to lock-keepers for every pig destroyed found grubbing there. Unlike the canal companies in England who often only had rights to the cut and the towpath, the Irish promoters owned strips of land on either side of the cut. Under nationalisation these passed into the hands of CIE. But before that time, when revenue dwindled, the canal company let portions of this land to farmers and even stretches of the line had grazing rights attached. This policy has been stopped as rights to grazing come up for renewal. Nevertheless some farmers are obliged to swim their cattle across since the Grand was built with very few accommodation bridges.

Our invaluable guide to the Grand Canal of Ireland, written by Ruth Delany, author of the definitive history of the cut, and Jeremy Addis and recently published by the IWAI, had another tale and although it concerned the village of Pollagh, a good three miles down the line, Walter was willing to confirm the story. It is said that St. Monachan cast a penance on Pollagh to the effect that the people had to supply free milk to travellers. The good saint was irate that some inhabitant of the village had stolen his cow and put it in the pot. "Today's traveller," comments the guide, "will probably have to pay, and even pay a deposit on the bottle." I thought that Walter was near enough to Pollagh to pay the penance so when it was time to leave I asked for the milk. He shook his head with a smile but offered a pint of Guinness in its place. If this is a new penance I'll take my hat off to it.

After bidding Walter farewell it was only two miles to what the guide describes as "a convenient quay making it difficult to pass The Thatch public house". We found it perfectly convenient, the more so since Brendan and John were already in the place. There was just enough room to moor astern of *Boyle Star*, which was fine until we discovered that the canal-side wall of the wharf shed was also used as the bar toilet, notwithstanding a perfectly good loo which had been installed inside the bar during modernisation. As

I've said of the area, old customs are retained. John McNamara lives and works in Tullamore, just a few miles away, and that evening we were joined by his wife Ann. Later we retired to raid *Boyle Star*'s cocktail cabinet and celebrate our first day on the canal.

On other occasions, when both our cellars had run dry, the terminal pint could be something of a problem. One incident caused a great deal of amusement. We were moored outside a bar with which John claimed to be well acquainted and having finished our drinks on the boat we all felt in need of that final draught. Time had long been called but John vanished into the darkness only to return a little later with an empty tray and a long face. What most upset our friend was that there were "a dozen of them in there drinking away". With that Brendan rose to his feet and marched off to the door returning equally quickly with brimful jars which he thrust suavely through the hatch as though he was serving Buck's Fizz on the *QE2*. In another establishment we heard that the owner had been very embarrassed to find that the night's takings, packed in a leather pouch, had been stolen. The discovery was not made until the bar closed and since this was a rare occasion, taking place at about three a.m., the good fellow had a hard time explaining why it was the wee sma' hours of the morning before he called the barracks.

TWELVE

The Morning Dew

TULLAMORE, THE FIRST TOWN we were to meet after more than twenty miles of canal travel, lay just over an hour ahead. Already Val and I had noticed that our passage along the cut was beginning to resemble similar journeys across England. Unlike the Shannon and the lakes, where we were happy to make landfall and traipse "inland" to discover the relics, history and legends of the place, here we were equally happy to let the canal dictate the course of our wanderings. Civilisations built themselves around the landscape of the Shannon; the canal was imposed by man across a landscape, creating as it went changes in the pattern of life. It was the history and tales of the canal with which we were most concerned, rather than that which had gone before.

The Grand Canal reached Tullamore in 1798 and an extensive series of warehouses and an hotel were built, along with a canal harbour reached by a short arm. Having negotiated the turn into the arm, the basin is entered by another perfect right-angle turn. If you make one mistake as you go into it you will find yourself sailing into John McNamara's office. No doubt every bend meant a few extra yards and a few extra pounds for the contractors. Such are the joys of canal travel. But our entry into Tullamore more than made up for the hazards within the town limits as we passed the two castles, Ballycowan and Sraa, which line the banks on the approach. The previous day's rain had not abated and we were both exceedingly damp as we locked up into the town and moored to the whiskey bond quay with its old crane still intact. The bonded ware-houses are still in use although their contents now depart by road and rail and this was where we were directed to the offices of D. E. Williams, makers of the famous Tullamore Dew brand of whiskey.

We introduced ourselves at the company offices and were graciously received by Eugene Spollen who invited us to view the buildings and, more important, sample "the product". First we were to discover that Tullamore Dew was now distilled in Dublin and that it was rarely to be seen in Ireland, the majority of the output being exported to Germany. Daniel Williams bought out a previous Tullamore distiller in 1885 but when a number of Irish distillers set up a united company the brand name was sold. The company still retains a licence to distil at Tullamore but has now diversified into the production of everything from broiler chickens to the legendary Irish Mist liqueur. Fortunately we were in the premises of the latter.

Malt and grain whiskeys are brought to Tullamore where secret processes transform honest whiskey into the mellowest of potions, holding in its heart "the blood of the sun as it slaughtered sank". You could fill a book with the lore which accompanies the making of this liqueur since although production began in 1948 the ante-cedents of Irish Mist go back to pre-Christian times, to the seasons of milk and mellow drunkenness when the national cup ran over, not with some fearsome poteen, but with the graceful sparkle of heather wine, a subtle blend of whiskey, herbs and heather honey. One of the earliest references to the spirit occurs in the Annals of Clonmacnois where we are told that a chief "died at Christmas by taking a surfeit of aqua vitae". According to our guide there was a doubtful recipe for this essence in the *Book of Durrow* which dates from around A.D. 900.

In spite of endless experiments Daniel Williams was never able to reproduce this "sustenance for gods and fighting men". Legend has it that the secrets of the distillation were lost during the Flight of the Wild Geese after the Battle of Aughrim. After years of trial and error, during which time the family must have suffered more hangovers than most, an Austrian came to Tullamore. Lo and behold should he not be of Irish descent and have in his hand the true recipe for the long-lost heather wine. To say that Eugene had a spirited twinkle in his eye when he told us this tale would be true enough, but whatever you may think of its authenticity, it is as original as the Irish Mist to which it relates.

Eugene led us through seas of liqueur and in the box store we saw consignments bound for more than one hundred and twenty countries. One of their most curious clients is the island of Nauru which, since it is only a few miles in circumference with a population of around 3,000, can only be found on very large maps. It had taken Irish Mist's marketing division some time to discover its location but if you put a ruler through Tokyo and line it up with Fiji it will pass through Nauru. The last order was for 120 cases with a dozen bottles in each case and since the order is frequently repeated official thinking is that the islanders bathe in the stuff.

The Pacific island is one of the richest republics, the great wealth of its inhabitants being based on the droppings of millions of prehistoric sea birds which has provided them with a phosphate-rich economy. Today the phosphate is running out but the Government's investment plans are likely to equal the phosphate earnings. The investment centre is already housed in a fifty-two-storey block in Melbourne, daubed bird-shit tower. According to one report the "prosperous paunchy islanders mainly sleep, fish and occasionally kill each other on Nauru's twelve-mile road system which is cluttered up with over 2,000 cars and motorcycles".

Tullamore derives from Tulach Mor, the great hill, and although the rising ground was not in evidence, a quick look at the canal map showing the eight-lock climb into and out of the town indicated that we were moving on to a new level. Our mooring for the night was to be at the only hire-cruiser base on the canal but before moving on we made the awkward turn into the canal harbour and lay alongside one of the old engineering barges. Down in the dry dock Mike and Heather Thomas, who run Celtic Cruisers from the old lock house at twenty-fourth lock, were scrubbing down their fleet in readiness for the coming season. While they got on with their work we explored the harbour and those buildings which have escaped the demolisher's hammer. The stately canal hotel was used as a

presbytery from 1859 until 1974 when it was reduced to rubble. The
new building is allegedly in keeping with the design of the old but
having seen photographs of that grand old building I can only
suppose that the suggestion is something of a joke.

All around us were piled new gates, each marked with the name
of the lock it was built for, along with balance beams and stacks of
the paraphernalia of the canal builder's art. A row of low work-
shops contained a small foundry and inside the largest shed the
skeleton frames of more gates lay on stout trestles. John McNamara's
office is one of the high spots of any trip and I recommend a visit.
You will be warmly welcomed but I suggest a telephone call to the
canal depot beforehand.

The office is a living museum with drawers and shelves packed
with relics of the cut in its heyday. There is a collection of several
hundred photographs dating from the beginning of this century,
many faded with age and with notes by the hand of some long-dead
engineer. They show the tugs which used to pull trains of boats
across the long bog levels, dredgers and weedcutters, locks working
and flooded by winter spates on the Barrow, and breaches which
have brought traffic to a standstill. Among the papers and pamphlets
was one which seemed to have little to do with canals, but no doubt
a learned treatise *On the Medicinal Properties of Pure Peat Moss
Carbonised* was of interest to more than just its author, a certain
Jasper W. Rogers CE, in the year 1853. One document of considerable historical value was a handwritten report by Christopher
Mulvany on the state of the Barrow between Athy and St. Mullins
in 1853. Mulvany was the company engineer from 1847 until his
death in 1895 in which time he undertook the repair of many
breaches. The problems on the Barrow navigation were quite
different to those on the canal, as we were to discover when we
reached Athy. Mulvany's report on dredging, blasting rock channels
and repairing weirs concluded with the astronomical estimate of
£239 8 shillings.

But pride of place in John's office must go to the roller maps
which hang around the walls like holland blinds in search of a
window. The largest of these is more than six feet high and twelve
feet long and includes a scale drawing of the Leinster Aqueduct

which carries the canal over the Liffey. Beneath the drawing the caption reads:

The Leinster Aqueduct is built over the River Liffey (near Sallins) in five feet of water subject to violent floods which rise to fifteen feet. The foundation is sunk seven feet through sand and gravel and large stones to strong blue clay. The whole river across has the same strata at equal depths. It was passable for boats in eighteen months from the day of laying the foundation, and cost £7,500.

Brendan and John only wish that every part of the buildings was as well described. Among other maps was a splendid set of the Barrow Navigation, hand made in colour by John Molloy in 1813.

There are those who may wonder why such important articles of canal history are not in a museum but in fact these maps and plans are still in regular use, along with the ancient and much altered land plans, as they give details of repairs, alterations, building works and land ownership which cannot be found elsewhere.

By the time we had completed our exploration of the Tullamore yard it was well past tea time and since we had been invited to join Mike and Heather Thomas that evening we decided to investigate the gastronomic joys of the town. The first café we arrived at described itself as a fish and chip emporium.

"What kind of fish do you have," I asked the girl behind the counter.

"Just fish," said she.

"Then I'll just have fish and chips for two."

When the fish arrived it was rectangular, some five inches long by two inches broad, and about an inch thick. Its flavour, like its shape, had nothing to do with the sea.

Returning to *Fenniscourt* we set out for twenty-sixth lock beside which stands an unusual double-storey lock house. The two-storey porch is crudely castellated and although the slate roof rises at front and rear in the traditional manner, the house gables do not extend up to the apex of the roof. Instead the slates curve round the side of the rounded end walls so that the whole affair sits on top of the residence like a great hat. No lock-keeper appeared but at twenty-fifth lock Mrs. Kelly was out and about and wielding her windlass with gay abandon. Although many of the wives assist at the locks if their husbands are in the fields there are only two women lock-keepers on the Grand Canal. Mike and Heather themselves helped us through the lock outside their home and we were soon sitting comfortably inside with an unusual choice of Irish or Scotch to ease the aches of a long, damp and tiring day.

Mike Thomas hails from Blackpool but his regard for Ireland is only bettered by his love for the canal and his four-craft fleet stems from his belief that the waterway has a future. There is a Freeman 22 and two venerable but elegant Broads cruisers which make a pleasant change from the glass fibre of the lakes. But his latest vessel is breaking new ground. *Celtic Lady* is an English canal narrow boat, built of steel and ideal for the canal since the slab sides, which are peculiar to these craft, make them steady in locks. There is one other splendid advantage. With a beam of only six feet ten inches *Celtic Lady* should pass through the broad locks of the Grand Canal with only one gate open. A lazy man's cruiser.

Next morning was fine as we made our way towards Robertstown, thirty miles and six locks to the east. Barely had we left for the first lock than Mrs. Kelly winged by on her Moped, one hand holding a lock key, the other giving us a cheerful wave, and her headscarf billowing forth in the slipstream. I could barely bring myself to watch her bucketing progress up the line. We were soon in the chamber and as we rose to the next level a battered heap of a car came down the line. The waterway telegraph in these parts is even better than that on the Shannon. God knows how Mrs. Kelly knew of our departure but I doubt if even she could tell how Michael Donoghue, whose house stands at twenty-first lock, knew we were approaching.

By the time we had reached Michael's lock, however, there was no sign of the man. In a field by his house we found his goat and kid and when Val and I approached the most curious event took place for the kid, rather than running towards his mother for protection, jumped on top of an ass which was lying on the grass. By the time we had fetched a camera to record this strange spectacle, the ass, of course, had got wearily to his feet and no amount of cajoling could persuade the stubborn beast to settle again. By this time Michael had arrived on Shank's pony with a dire tale. His car had failed him. This was no ordinary car but a £10 banger which he had converted to run on liquid gas. Having got over this wound to his engineering pride, a process assisted by a small nip from *Fenniscourt*'s cellars, Michael decided to make up for his failure by telling us his life story. It was an excellent tale.

"I started work as the greaser, the cabin boy, on my father's boat and I can tell you the very day it was for it was the coldest, wettest, most snarling day of the year. It was St. Stephen's Day, 1934. My father was working the boats and it was natural that I should join him. There were four of us and we'd all work her through Dublin and then the master and greaser took shifts with the crewmen. We were going twenty-four hours a day. It was hard for you'd never sleep right in the bow cabin and when the stop man misjudged the rope length to the bollard on the lockside we'd ram the gates and if you were in bed at the time you shot out bloody fast, perpendicular. Either that or they'd open the damned racks too fast and you'd be half drowned. We were working porter from St. James's to Limerick and we'd take about six days on the round trip. Then we'd have twenty-four hours at home. Most of the boatmen lived around Lowtown so we'd try to be sure we arrived there on our rest day.

"I remember we were working through Ardnacrusha and for some reason the lock-keeper was away. I got ashore and went to find him and as we came back to the river he told me about two fine salmon which were lying in a pool at the bottom of the empty locks. I was a kid at the time and wanted to fetch them up. Fine, says he. What I didn't think about was the hundred foot or so of slimy steel ladder which was the only way to the bottom of the chamber. But I made it. But the going up was terrible for the bloody fish were vast and I was frightened that with all their flapping around I'd be flung to the concrete."

Here I asked Michael why he hadn't killed the fish before climbing to the lockside.

"Do you think I'm bloody mad as well as greedy. I wasn't staying down there a minute more than I needed to with all that water waiting to come in and your man with his hand on the button. Anyway I made it and we ate salmon for breakfast, lunch and dinner for three days and we were sick to death of the stuff by the end of it. There's not a salmon here but I'm told there's a pike or two about. Not that I've seen one myself for a day or two."

During the Second World War Michael left the canal to work his turf bank, sending fuel to Dublin in specially-commissioned wooden boats which were brought into service to beat the fuel shortage. Then he worked for Irish River Floatels as captain of one of the hotel boats which once plied the Shannon. One of these craft, converted from a Shannon tug and supply boat, was the *St. Patrick*, built in 1935 and used on the Severn Navigation before being brought to Ireland. Michael vanished into his house and returned with a great collection of photographs of those days when he sported a fine bit of gold braid for the benefit of the tourists.

A little way past Michael's house is the reed-blocked entrance to the Kilbeggan Branch of the canal which ran for eight lock-free miles to the town of that name. It was closed in 1961 and Michael could only remember having passed that way once in a working boat. Crossing the roving bridge over the derelict branch we passed along the line to Chevenix Bridge where there is a pleasant bar and grocery, and a quay which would provide a quiet but victualled mooring for those who want to avoid the towns and villages where the entire population tends to promenade of an evening to view the yachts, as the people who live by the canal call everything other than an old barge. No one could explain how this term had come about. Did some Victorian gentleman take his steam yacht through the canal? It certainly was not *Phoenix* from Lough Derg since her draught is too great.

The houses of Daingean, site of the 1975 breach, broke the solitude of this part of our voyage for a few moments but soon we were out again on to the bog. We passed through the area known to the boatmen as The Red Girls, after a family of auburn-haired beauties who lived nearby. The spot is marked today by a bright yellow low level lifting railway bridge which carries turf to a nearby power station. It rose as we approached, its balance beams dipping into the canal, for the tracks are carried out from the bank on piles

Milford drawbridge, giving access to the island formed by canal and river. The lock and lockhouse are in the background.

The Black Castle at Leighlin-bridge.

Muine Bheag drawbridge and lock, and serene waters before re-entering the Barrow.

Clashganny lock and weir two miles north of Graiguenamanagh. Skippers coming downstream need to keep a sharp lookout for the unmarked weir which follows a blind bend and is completely unguarded. The two water channels which enter below the lock throw up a confusing silt bar.

and the opening section is barely wide enough to let a full width canal boat through.

The town of Edenderry is approached by the only navigable branch of the canal. Turning left into the arm we passed under the roving bridge which carries the line and were amazed at the narrowness of the structure which surely would never have passed a well-fed boat horse. The one-mile branch and its harbour were built privately, by Lord Devonshire, and completed in 1802. Today the harbour has been pleasantly landscaped with seats and tubs of flowers. It stands high above the bustling main street and it was a curious sensation to descend to road level. We managed to arrive just as the school was coming out, and, of course, every child in the town soon heard that a yacht had come. We had been warned of vandalism and theft from boats moored in the larger towns, the same problem which afflicts craft on English waterways, but we never encountered any such trouble. Instead the children seemed moved more by curiosity. It was, however, a little disconcerting when one young lady of not too tender years stuck her hand through the window and heaved back the curtains of the loo while I was standing there minding my own business. I suspect that she was equally put out by the event. After taking on water and a jar at Mary O'Connor's hospitable Harbour Bar, where a flock wallpaper salesman has done a roaring trade, we left once more for the Shannon Line.

The short stretch between Edenderry and the Blundell Aqueduct has suffered four breaches and when we reached the aqueduct we went to explore this vast embankment which rises some twenty feet or more above the surrounding land. The road passage beneath the canal is known locally as The Tunnel. It's a great leaking cavern of a place and not to be dallied in. As we climbed back to the line an elderly gentleman appeared with his dog and bade us good evening. It was a happy encounter for this was Joe Moore, one-time canal inspector and a man with an excellent memory of the waterway in its heyday. Joe took to the boats in the twenties.

"When I was first offered employment by the Grand Canal Company I was to work on a steam dredger on the River Barrow. I arrived just before eight in the morning and was promptly handed a shovel, but as I couldn't see much use for a shovel in the middle of a river I put it down and lit a cigarette. A voice from the cabin window announced that there would be no smoking while on duty. I thought to myself that I wouldn't be long at this caper and stuffed the butt in my pocket. That was more years ago than I care to remember. Well, I was twenty-five years on the dredgers and thirty years a canal inspector. I was engaged to be married and the roving life of a boatman was not the sort of thing I wanted for my family and that was how I got the inspector's job."

The canal company built a neat bungalow for their new man at Edenderry, just below the embankment where all the breaches had occurred, but this did not seem to spoil the newly weds' pleasure at having a home of their own. My assumption that Joe had retired was quickly corrected. Only the winter before, while minding a pump on the line, he had fallen into the pit of a backdrain and, unable to climb out, had spent the night there. Brendan was later to assure me that no man would ever persuade Joe Moore to forsake his beloved canal. You could tell from Joe's conversation that inspectors were a cut above the average canal employee. He wore a heavy wool weave jacket, trousers and waistcoat and his stick was more a symbol of status than infirmity. As though to prove the point he insisted on taking us on a conducted tour of the old breaches and there was a catch in his throat as he described the dog he had once, a fine bitch who would bring his cows a full mile up the line for milking without him even setting foot over the door. Prince, who lay at his feet, has neither the opportunity nor the intelligence to perform such a feat.

"He's the bane of my life," said Joe. But there was a twinkle in his eye and a biscuit in his hand when he said it.

"I can remember the harbour in Dublin when it was flitting with men like flies. And now what is there? They've filled it with concrete. And look at the canal now. We're lucky to see one yacht a week and the old boats come hardly at all. They call it progress. They don't know the meaning of the word. It's a poor country and it's a poorer one that can't fit its ways to its means. Are you telling me it cost too much to take the porter to Limerick by boat. And the other stuff as well. It cost hardly anything in boats and diesel. And those roads cost a lot more to maintain than the canal.

They're all full of potholes. But the canal is sound to this day."

By now the sun had sunk low in the west but the amber of its fall was strewn among the clouds and the waters were tinged with the colour. We had often read of the Irish light, a cliché of the tourist manuals. It is not. We wished to stay longer with Joe but if we were to catch up with Brendan and John it was essential that we reached Robertstown that night. There was something else in the stillness which beckoned us to continue and our passage that evening was one of the most gentle moments of our voyage. We said our farewells and Joe stood at the narrow stone edged point where the water channel passes over the road and waved us into infinity. One more lock and we were on the great Bog of Allen. This was infinity, a wilderness "surcharged and swol'n up like a sponge".

The night drew on until the stars stood like jewels in the gloaming and we could barely make out the shape of the occasional building as we passed. The silence was disturbed for a moment as we came abreast of a clanking floodlit factory and two men waved from the bank. Then on into the gathering night. In spite of the surrounding bog the water grew clearer as we progressed and the bed of the cut seemed coated with a bluey-white clay. In the moonlight our passage ahead was gently lit. As we moved up to nineteenth lock, at Lowtown, between neatly-moored boats lining Ted Barrett's boatyard, a voice hailed us from the bank. A friendly walker perhaps. When we reached the lock the voice turned out to belong to Frank Blake who, with his wife Gay, was preparing *Francielle* for the Athy Rally. Frank is a member of the Dublin Branch of the IWAI and we had met on an earlier trip. They came on board for a noggin before setting out for their Dublin home and by the time they had departed it was too dark to continue.

To the boat crew passing towards Dublin from the Shannon the nineteenth lock marks the start of the summit level of the Grand Canal which lies 279 feet above sea level. Mrs. Conroy is the lockkeeper. The chamber is similar to any other but it contains a curiously sited fuelling point which I have seen nowhere else. The flexible hose lies in a channel cut into one of the stone walls which, in the days of the working boats, would have allowed craft to refuel while passing through the lock, instead of losing time mooring at a

separate quay. Above and below the lock a channel leads to the
Barrow Line of the Grand Canal, the older of these leading from the
summit level having been restored in 1973. From now on we would
be moving "downhill", theoretically an easier passage, since craft
in a falling lock do not require to put ropes ashore; for some reason
beyond my understanding, water flowing out of a lock keeps a craft
stationary in the chamber. Perhaps it works the opposite way round
in Australia.

Before entering the Barrow Line we continued along the summit
level for a little under a mile to reach the village of Robertstown.
Here is a settlement which resembles closely the English canal
villages of Sutton Stop, meeting place of the Coventry and Oxford
canals, and Stoke Bruerne on the Grand Union. Houses and old
stores line the banks which form a continuous wharf through the
village. But it is the approach to Robertstown from the west which
provides the most stunning view as you round a gentle curve before
Binn's Bridge and see, framed in the stone arch, the bulk of the
Grand Canal Company's hotel. The building has been refurbished,
painted, re-roofed and houses a permanent exhibition of canal and
local interest, thanks to the enthusiasm of the local community
guild, Muintir na Tire, the IWAI and the Georgian Society. It won
a restoration award in the Council of Europe Architectural Heritage
Year, 1975. Today the canalside cobbles still ring to the sound of
iron shoes as the guild's horse-drawn barges get under way. Each
year the village celebrates with the Robertstown Festa, two weeks of
singing, eating, dancing and boating centred round the hotel in which
traditional banquets are held. Run by local people, I was assured
that they avoided the worst excesses of commercially-operated
ancient banquets. All was quiet during the few hours we remained
in Robertstown and the only interruption was when a local farmer
herded his cattle along the quay. It was the first time we had seen
a cowherd perform his duties from the seat of a Moped.

The water on which we rested enters the canal from the Milltown
Feeder which carries the outpourings of springs near Pollardstown.
It must be spoken of with reverence. Not only are there seven
springs, known as St. James's Well, but this is the true source of
Arthur Guinness's beverage. There are some people who still

believe that Guinness owes its vitality to the waters of the Liffey but were they to visit Dublin and pass over O'Connell Bridge at low tide they would be sorely hurt to see their romantic dream flow by, a sluggish, stinking sea of effluent. I heard tell once of a member of the Guinness family who boasted greatly of what Guinness had done for Ireland until one day he was rebuked by a friend who reminded him of what Ireland had done for Guinness. In truth, the great brewery has done much for the Grand Canal since its demand for the pure water of St. James's Well makes the waterway one of the cleanest cuts in the world. Even weedkillers are banned from the summit to Dublin lest they interfere with that taste of goodness.

The mechanical working of the bogs has transformed many areas of the country as, denuded of its ground cover, the land lies bare and lifeless. Many birds and small animals moved to places where their food supply and protective cover still stood. But an even greater transformation is taking place as the worked out bogs are reclaimed. The terrain on the opening stretches of the Barrow Line has recently been planted with conifers and, since Ireland has the fastest tree growth in Europe, it will not be long before the canal traveller cruises between an avenue of greenery. At Rathangan we left the bog.

Many of the towns and villages on the Barrow Line have gone to considerable lengths to make the canal's passage through their boundaries an attractive one and neat lawns and wayside seats, with even a town nameplate, marked our passage round Rathangan. The signs were useful since we had left the Ordnance Survey maps to this part of our journey in London. It is a different story at the locks. One in particular had us bustling through as fast as possible. All round the lock was a litter of animal bones, some with a good deal of flesh still attached. Two enormous dogs ran on a roving chain which allowed them to get within a few feet of where we were working through and having reached the end of their tether, they reared ferociously on their hind legs and bayed. The Baskerville hound had nothing on those two and when we passed this foul place and found a small white cross on the bank we wondered just what kind of tragedy had taken place.

After Rathangan there were two double locks, one of which sported the customary inconvenient bridge. This one had been built so close to the gates that channels had been cut in the inside face of the arch to receive the balance beams and allow the gates to open fully. I thought at the time that the eccentricities of the bridge-builders were limitless, as to have constructed the bridge a few more yards away from the lock itself would have been little trouble. On our return to London, however, Val came up with an idea which may well account for this curious arrangement at the lock. A bridge built across the chamber uses the sturdy lock walls and their foundations as its base. To have extended the chamber or built separate foundations would have added to the expense of the works. Perhaps there was method to the construction after all.

Our efforts were rewarded for we were now entering the valley of the River Barrow. What we could see of the countryside through an ever-present curtain of drizzle was rolling and luxuriant. Monas-terevan was the next large town and as we rounded a bend we came upon a Triffid-like construction barring our progress. At one time the canal terminated at this town and boats locked down into the river to continue to Athy. Then the canal was extended but craft still locked down, crossed the river, and locked back up again. In 1829 this time-wasting procedure was overcome by the construction of an aqueduct and it was then that Monasterevan's bascule bridge was built.

Since the bridge carries a busy road, it is kept locked and enquiries at a nearby house provided the information that the key was kept by the lock-keeper on the other side of the aqueduct. After a small commotion with the keeper's terrier, who made up for his lack of size with a darting pincer movement accompanied by a wild snapping and yapping, I managed to knock on the door. It was opened by the keeper's wife and when I asked if the bridge might be raised she stood back in considerable shock.

"Why, there's never a yacht wanting by?" she exclaimed.

Since I was standing before her with half the lock-beam tar of the Barrow Line smeared across my face and hands I didn't think her question required a reply.

The lady vanished into the nether regions of the house from which a disembodied conversation was to be heard.

"The man says he's got a yacht for going through the bridge."

"A yacht?"

"He wants to pass through the bridge."

"But there's already been a yacht through the bridge today."

The rain was getting heavier and the dog was getting nearer but eventually, after a great deal more muttering about all the yachts in Ireland wanting to pass through Monasterevan in one day Joe Moore's brother, Jim, appeared.

"Are you wanting to pass through the bridge?"

"Whenever you're ready," said I, thinking we would be lucky to get through this side of Christmas.

With that Jim vanished into the house to re-emerge with a great coterie of children and off we set down the line and across the aqueduct like Pied Piper's parade.

Jim wields his authority over the road traffic of Monasterevan with great panache. First there is the closing of the gates. This is followed by a conversation about the dangers of the job.

"Only the other day a flaming tractor ran right into the gate and if it hadn't been for the chain fence hanging from the bars there'd be another holy cross along the line. They all sit in their cars tootin' their horns as though all the bloody town was going to a wedding and never think of giving Jim a hand. That's why we have the children around."

This was a new light on the socio-economic behaviour of canal employees but it was of no interest at all to the motorists who by now lined the road on both sides of the bridge.

"There's other ways through, you know," said Jim. "Now we'll get things moving. Just a wee bit for a start 'cause it's heavy, you know."

Springs tightened, cogs met, hawsers straightened and with a shudder the bridge began to lift. Jim frequently stopped the procedure to have a breather and we all held on to the windlasses for fear that the thing might suddenly drop back.

"Now I think you have enough room, sir," said Jim.

"I think it's a bit close yet, Jim."

Reluctantly he helped to heave it up another two notches.

"You'd get the *Queen Mary* through there now," announced our friend, who promptly sat down on a bollard to emphasise his point.

At that moment a great commotion came from the other side of the canal. A herd of cattle were passing down the queue of cars and some of them had found the wing mirrors handy flea scrapers. Men stood on the bank alternately cursing canals and pleading for the proceedings to be hurried along. I for my part was equally intent on bow-hauling *Fenniscourt Star* through the gap since Jim's idea of headroom seemed to suggest that he'd be the better for a new pair of glasses. Somehow we made it, but that's only half the story. What goes up comes down. What goes up slowly comes down equally slowly.

Three hours later we locked into the canal harbour at Athy, a widened portion of the cut flanked by warehouses and wharves. A magnificently converted canal boat was moored here and, astern of her, lay *Boyle Star*. We were introduced to Brendan's wife, Peggy, who had joined him for the evening and later to Rusty and George Speirs who had carried out the conversion on the former canal boat, 95B. Rusty and George are leading lights of the IWAI in Athy and I mean them no injustice when I say that this is hardly surprising since there appears to be only three members of the association in the town. They had organised a boat rally in the harbour for the following weekend and before our departure next day invitations were issued and accepted.

Nothing now lay between us and the River Barrow but a bank. Ruth and Jeremy's strip guide to the Grand has a key showing the site of everything from golf courses to water points. But it does not show any banks and our store of filthy lucre had dwindled to a few pence on our way down the Barrow Line. Irish banks are a little like Irish miles and owe something to the imagination. Some were closed when we arrived, others opened on one day each week which was never the day of our visit. Elsewhere complicated notices announced the arrival of a travelling bank at certain times on certain days. It wasn't until we reached Athy that, as Brendan put it, the crew of *Fenniscourt Star* found a stationary bank.

THIRTEEN

Troubled Waters

But yet on one side a goodley river called the Barro fleeteth throughout the whole countrie that upon it they so conveighe all their comodyties and merchaundyses from the seas or from Waterford even to the house at Laghlyn which house standathe full upon the said river.

THE RIVER BARROW is the second longest river in Ireland, running for one hundred and nineteen miles from its source in the Slieve Bloom Mountains on Barna (1,659 feet) until it mingles its waters, first with the Nore and then with the Suir, to enter the estuary of Waterford Harbour, passing into the sea between Hook Head and the fishing village of Dunmore East. Like the Shannon the Barrow is long enough to have cast up many legends along its course and there is one from its very source. It is said that if any man should gaze at the spring well that is the source of this river the waters will flood and cause devastation to the surrounding land. The only way of avoiding catastrophe is to say Mass on the spot. It would seem that the religious inclinations of the people are sadly lacking for the floods of the Barrow are notorious.

Today the navigable portion of canalised river runs for forty-two miles from Athy to the sea lock at St. Mullins. From there to New Ross navigation is dependent on the tide but below the port a dredged channel is always open. Below Athy we were able to cruise with some geographical certainty since we had Ordnance Survey maps to the area and it was easy to see that the scenic wonders of the Barrow might come to pass. The valley is never more than a few miles wide, the green shading on the map quickly giving way to darker browns as the water cuts its way to the sea.

Bill Duggan, a Carlow solicitor and ardent member of the IWAI, provided us with the sixteenth-century quotation at the beginning of this chapter. It comes from the *Life and Times of Sir Peter Carew*. The Barrow certainly "fleeteth" but its "goodley" qualities as a navigation are more doubtful. A slate bed, innumerable rapids, vicious currents and winter floods which send silt banks roving around the waterway to confuse low-level summer passage, are just a few of the hazards with which the navigation's engineers had to contend. A still-water canal would have solved all those problems but it was decided to use the river for much of the route.

The result is an eccentric waterway the like of which we had never encountered. An unmarked boat stream, blasted out of the river bed, passing along one bank and then along the other, must be held to if you are not to run aground. This comes from the newsletter of the IWAI:

Member Simon Nolan warns Barrow navigators to take the dotted line course on the Barrow Branch's duplicated charts very literally. Two hundred yards south of Milford Lock at Easter he wasn't as close to the west bank as he should have been, as he now knows to his cost. With only two feet draught his marine ply boat *Special Kay* was badly holed by what might have been a tree trunk in mid stream.

At least our unfortunate skipper was spared contact with the wandering boulder of Barrowmount, a legendary obstacle which seems to roll in and out of the boat stream depending on its mood. Bill Duggan has his own thoughts on the matter. He has always kept up a friendly rivalry with Jimmy Gill, a CIE employee and Barrow boatman. Jimmy maintains that the rock has been there since the flood. Bill wonders which flood he means since he has not actually hit the rock himself. It has been said that rivalry between the pair is such that one of Jimmy's supporters manhandles the boulder out of the river whenever Bill is around. It is back again by the time the next yacht passes by and so Bill's authority has, quite literally, a hole knocked in it.

Bill's chart of the river served us well but whether by luck or judgment we shall not know until we once more make our way down the boatstream. His notes are excellent but the cartography leaves the course a little uncertain. "Boat stream changes from west bank to east bank here", announces the legend. Just where "here" is can be difficult to guess since the instructions seem to cover a good half-inch of the drawing which lacks a precise scale.

If the boat stream doesn't get yon then beware of sand in your weed filter. Nasty one, that. In order to overcome the falls the engineers constructed a series of canals running parallel to the river. At the head of each cut a weir traverses the river and at the tail a lock gives access back into the boat stream. Result? While much of the silt and debris is passed over the weir, that which is not runs into the cut. Below the lock the fast-flowing river tends to build up a bar. Regular and expensive dredging has always been required. We picked up a pipeful of silt once and spent a frenzied hour clearing it. Why is it that boat engines are always installed in such a way that you would need a dozen more articulations in your arms to get at them?

The hazards were somewhat alleviated by the helpfulness of the people we met along the line and before we parted from John and Brendan at Muine Bheag, they marked some of the problems which did not appear on the chart. Not only did they not appear on the chart but they were even at odds with the printed instructions. John happily marked in a silt shoal at the very point where the chart warned that the course was only a few feet from the bank. It was the kind of information we were pleased to receive, even if it did mean that Val spent much of her time perched on the bows scanning the depths for sandbanks, trees and wandering boulders.

One Barrow obstacle which is easily avoided yet seems an unnecessary hindrance is the great tree of Bahana Wood. The trunk, complete with branches piled high with flotsam and jetsam, lies spreadeagled across the stream. In a few years there will be a completely new island based around the tree. The guide notes the hazard: "Large tree for many years in boatstream—it is quite safe to pass outside it."

It was, then, with a certain amount of trepidation that we shot out of twenty-eighth lock and scuttled across river to the entrance to the Ardreigh Canal which lies on the opposite bank. Upstream an elegant many-arched bridge framed the river's unnavigable course. Downstream the arches of a railway bridge complicated the entrance to the canal while the water pouring down the Barrow did everything it could to sweep us on to the weir. Thankfully we made the entrance. Our voyage down the Barrow had begun.

The canals which bypass the river rapids are tranquil oases between the swirling waters of the boat stream. At first the scenery was gentle and undulating as we passed along the channels of Ardreigh and Levitstown with forests of wild cherry and fuchsia trailing down to the water's edge. Levitstown cut is the longest on the river, running for more than two miles. At its end a simple lifting bridge gives road access to a splendid castellated maltings of which only the skeleton remains, the roof and wood-clad interior having gone up in yet another of Ireland's mysterious fires. Beyond the bridge lies the lock but before we could pass through, a gentleman from the house which lies in the shadow of the maltings appeared and invited us to a sup of home-brewed ale.

Mr. Jeffreys was something of a do-it-yourself enthusiast. Years ago he would have been thought of as an eccentric. Today he is just a very practical man. As we walked towards the house we passed over two culverts running from the canal. The first of these led to an ingeniously slatted eel trap from which many stones of this excellent Barrow delicacy are taken each year. The second took another supply of water to his private generating station which supplies the house with electricity.

The garden into which we were led had the qualities of another age, more fitted to the orchard lanes of Kent than a nation where gardening has for long taken second place to the essentials of good husbandry. A quince tree was trained along a wall, the flame-coloured blossom contrasting delightfully with the old weathered stone. Night-scented stocks and wallflowers abounded and the roses

might have surprised Harry Wheatcroft. Dogs, an essential orna-
ment of the grand manner of gardens, bounded everywhere. In this
elegant setting we got down to sampling the product of Mr. Jeffreys'
brewhouse, available on draught from the barrel or in bottled form.
Both were of excellent bouquet and fine clarity, and neither owed
anything to instant beer kits, but were the result of much painstaking
labour with malt, hops, yeast and water. Had the maltings not been
long deceased, Guinness might have had a worthy rival on the banks
of the Barrow.

Time came and went but eventually Brendan, who had assumed
the role of admiral of our tiny fleet, consulted his chronometer and
announced that it was time to set sail. As we continued down river
Val put the finishing touches to a magnificent bœuf en daube.
Having caught up with Brendan and John it was our intention to
feast them in the manner to which, judging by the meal we had
consumed at Banagher, they were accustomed. The slow cooking
casserole was too much for John. *Boyle Star* was running astern of
us at the time and the succulent aroma wafting from our galley had
set up the kind of hunger pangs which only lunch would subdue.

It was during lunch that a terrible fate beset us. A sharp report
from the galley signalled the end of all Val's labours as the oven-
ware casserole exploded. Later we heard that glass breaking for no
apparent reason was a common occurrence on heavily-powered
cruisers, the constant vibration causing some kind of glass fatigue.
There was even a story of wine glasses breaking apart on the table.
None of this did anything to comfort Val at the demise of our
dinner. The next large town where supplies could be obtained was
Carlow. It was, naturally, early closing day but after much searching
Val returned to *Fenniscourt* with a ham shank. No substitute for
bœuf en daube, but food nevertheless.

The lock-keeper at Carlow, Michael Webster, became quite
excited at the sight of two yachts passing down the river. In the last
two days three yachts had passed through, the busiest three days of
the year and that, he proclaimed, was how it should be. Michael
cycled along the track between Bestfield and Carlow lock. At one
point a great waving and shouting broke out from the bank. It
seemed that *Fenniscourt Star* had failed to take note of the boat

stream which wandered from one bank to the other just below the vast Carlow sugar refinery, the first and largest in Ireland. The stench as we passed the factory outfall did nothing for John's appetite. An array of water samples now littered *Boyle Star*'s saloon and I would dearly like to know the result of the test water from the Carlow stretch of the Barrow.

It was a dull, dark and dismal afternoon by the time we reached Carlow, the sun having gone into mourning at the death of our dinner. To add to our woes *Boyle Star* had picked up some kind of twine on her propeller and John was feeling dull, dark and dismal, and a bit wet by the time he had cut it free. The town itself glowered over the river. In spite of its early historical importance as a border fortress, garrisoned soon after the Norman landing and changing hands frequently thenceforth, the town's eighteenth- and nineteenth-century development has left it with a very functional appearance. It boasts the first electric street lighting in Ireland but keeps quiet about the fate dealt out to some of its ancient buildings.

No doubt Dr. Parry Middleton thought he was providing the citizenry with an essential service when he decided to establish an asylum in the town in the early nineteenth century. The good doctor chose a peculiar building in which to house his patients, none other than the much-altered but still considerable castle built by Hugh de Lacey about 1180. Finding that the structure did not quite suit his needs Dr. Middleton stuffed the place with gunpowder and Bedlam it must have been on the day he lit the fuse in an attempt to reduce the place to more manageable proportions. Where many great soldiers had failed the doctor succeeded.

At Carlow bridge the river showed its teeth once more. With less than three inches between her cabin roof and the arch, *Boyle Star*'s burgee mast was neatly topped. Our own headroom was similar and we spent a few anxious moments negotiating the navigation arch. Once through, we moved back to the west bank for the entrance to Carlow lock where the prospect of the river greatly improved. Great mills towered above us and the white water of the weir brought colour to the scene along with Michael Webster's brightly-painted lock and the flowerbeds and trellising he has managed to establish on the tiny island between lock and weir. Below the lock a silt bar has formed and we both rose across this with a mighty thwack, thankful that it was sand and not rock we had struck.

By now the Barrow was developing into one of the most magnificent waterways we had ever travelled. Great swards of grassland swept to the waterside in a multitude of greens and the meadows were sprinkled with the confetti of buttercups. Beyond them the hills rose to shelter the valley. Even the overcast purple skies added majesty to the scene as we passed through Milford Lock where a collection of maltings of even greater proportions but equal dereliction to those at Levitstown stand on the island formed by the canal. A stud farm here produces some of the finest Irish horses to grace the turf.

Our destination that evening was the town of Leighlinbridge where we sat down to a lesser repast than that which we had planned. Afterwards we found one of those old Irish bars where the merriment matched the stout. In the morning, after an early night, we were better able to appreciate the beauty of our mooring outside a former maltings upstream of the bridge which is the oldest on the navigation. Built in 1320 and widened in the eighteenth century it carries the old highway from Dublin to the south which even today is a busy thoroughfare with traffic plummeting down a steep hill on the west bank to reach the crossing. Immediately below the bridge on the east bank stand the remains of the Black Castle. Like Carlow the fort was established by the Normans and became an important stronghold on the borders of the English Pale which ran down the Barrow to Waterford. Razed and rebuilt on more than one occasion it was eventually destroyed by Cromwellian troops.

Leighlinbridge is a large settlement with little evidence of factories to provide employment. The empty shells of the maltings — there were once seven here — bear witness to a busy past when the principal cargo of the boats on the Barrow was malt. Gerard D'Arcy, in his *Portrait of the Grand Canal*, makes an interesting distinction between the Barrow Men and the canal-boat crews. It appears that not only did the Barrow Men consider themselves more important than the average canal steerer but that this superiority was acknowledged by the Grand Canal Company who purchased control of the river from the Barrow Navigation Company in 1894. Barrow Men could travel anywhere on the system but canal employees were only permitted on the Barrow with a pilot. This may have been less a restrictive practice – the Grand's owners were notoriously anti-union – than a sensible expedient due to the churlish nature of the river.

Passing one of the old maltings on our way to explore the village we were surprised to notice that much of the machinery was still intact. A trolley by a window was adorned with the manufacturer's plate: "Malt Barrow No. 8 Bury St. Edmunds." Walking up the hill on the west bank we found the Catholic church of St. Lazerian and were taken aback by the bell tower which stands apart from the main building. It was not its position which surprised us but the angle at which the tower was poised. The leaning town of Leighlinbridge. A gentleman was tending the grounds and, anxious to discover more of this strange edifice, I enquired as to its history.

There was little to be discovered since records of the original buildings had been destroyed in a fire at the bishop's house at Braganza. He did know that the tower post-dated the church. Today the bell is rung by pulling on a cable which runs down the outside of the tower but our friendly informant insisted that the structure was quite safe and proceeded to lead us to its top. Four hundred feet later we emerged beneath the open bell, cast in Dublin in 1882, and had a magnificent view of the Barrow valley. I have my own theory about the tower although I would not like to put a date on its construction. It closely resembles an ornamented version of the round towers at Clonmacnois and on Lough Derg and it would seem likely that the architect had these in mind when he drew his plans. The walls were a full three feet thick and the stairs were granite blocks. Originally the bell was sheltered by a canopy supported by four pillars but these were removed and a simple open structure took their place. The pillars are now strewn around the grounds and the stone ball which topped off the tower makes a handy garden ornamemt.

Muine Bheag or Bagenalstown lay three miles downstream. Walter Bagenal had great designs for the settlement which was "to be of considerable architectural pretensions and to bear the name Ver-

An idyllic mooring on the Barrow at Graiguenamanagh. The bridge is typical of many of the beautiful river crossings.

John Weaving.

Walter Mitchell, lock-keeper on the Grand Canal.

Michael Donoghue, former Grand Canal boatman and lock-keeper.

sailles". When the coach road was re-routed Bagenal's plans came to nothing although the town took the family name. In 1924 the town was given an older name of Muine Bheag. A later survey to discover whether the inhabitants were happy with this change was inconclusive and so today the place is known officially as Muine Bheag but always referred to as Bagenalstown.

Whatever Bagenal's pretensions the result now is a neat and pleasant community rising gently from the quayside in a series of terraces. There is a delightful square filled with colour-washed houses and an abundance of shops. The church of St. Andrew jars the eye, the stonework being too brash and the entire building out of all proportion to the surrounding architecture. It is set back from the street and a high wall of similar stone juts out from the side of the church along the gable end of the terraced houses as though to hide them from view when looking at the church. The result is truly weird for windows break the wall in places where, presumably, the houses had windows before it was built. The courthouse, still used on the second Tuesday of every month, has a vast Doric portico which looks out on the river.

Returning to the quay we were met with a sight which we had never before seen in Ireland for although we had seen many tinkers, or itinerants as they are known, camped by the wayside in everything from modern caravans to crude canvas shacks, we had not come across a traditional horse-drawn home. Here, however, was a tinker family on the move. First came a donkey cart with mother and some children. Then a dozen asses. Next came the *pièce de résistance*, a traditional caravan with the great hooped cabin gaily painted and the father at the reins. A couple of fine-looking piebalds came next, ridden bareback by two older children, and bringing up the rear there was another donkey cart with a goat and dog attached by heavy chains.

The entire assembly stopped by the grass verge and without more ado the goat was flung over the retaining wall and into the canal on the end of a piece of rope. It was all the animal could do to move upstream to where the bank was lower and so make his way back on to dry land. The poor beast was apparently treated to similar dousings whenever the family passed running water, but whether this was an attempt to rid the creature of its stench or in accordance with some ancient custom we were not to discover. A friendly neighbourhood garda arrived on a motorcycle and hustled the family on their way with a seemingly pointless vigour.

During the afternoon we noticed a great deal of bustle at the lock below our mooring and it wasn't long before *Boyle Star* was to be seen rising in the chamber. Brendan and John had continued some way downstream and were now returning their boat to Muine Bheag at the end of their inspection trip. Val provided a splendid array of scones and cakes for all and then it was farewell until we returned to Athy and the boat rally in a week's time. Tommy Nolan, the lock-keeper, came with us as we passed through the lock beside Lodge Mills and on down to Fenniscourt where he lives and after which our boat was named. Tommy is proud of the river and provides a safe mooring for craft moving in stages up or downstream. His lock and gardens are a pleasure to see and we were not surprised to hear that he had won the Barrow Award in Bord Fáilte's lock-keepers' competition.

The Award scheme — there are separate ones for the Shannon and Grand — was received with a degree of amusement by members of the IWAI, who felt that while the scheme's intentions were fine, the bureaucratic thunderings about what would and would not bring pleasure to the judges were a mite restrictive to the charming follies, quirks and hobbies of individual keepers. Grass, announced Bord Fáilte, should not be treated as if it were a bowling green, nor broken up with flowerbeds or shrubs, which were to be in pots, tubs or hanging baskets. The IWAI thought this the beginning of some national standard and suggested, with good humour, that lock users might compensate the losers with an extra tip for the most splendid display of plastic gnomes, rainbow cottages and natty rosebeds where they would come as a surprise to the backward-walking stop rope man.

Below Fenniscourt the Barrow took on an even grander aspect as the hills closed in on the twisting stream and it was easy to see how this river had been likened to the Rhine in recent publicity. We discovered an advertisement, however, for the Great Southern and Western Railway of 1891 which showed that the first river to be

daubed the Irish Rhine was the River Blackwater. First the Black-
stairs Mountains came into view above the valley some seven miles
to the east, the great ridge dividing Carlow from Wexford and
running south from Mount Leinster (2,610 feet). Alas the demand
for better television reception has led some misguided body to
top off the mountain with a tall television relay mast which
might do wonders for Coronation Street but little for the landscape.

Sliguff cut was one of the most badly-silted canals we had encountered but we ploughed through and on to Upper Ballyellen
Lock. A limeworks stands by the chamber and everything, from the
grass to the ratchet of the racks, was covered in a layer of fine dust.
It made the gear hard to work but at the sound of our engine a group
of men appeared from the factory and bent their bums to the beams
so that we were through without difficulty.

Passing beneath the road crossing at Goresbridge we saw the
original river wharf on the west bank but since this was out of the
boat stream we decided not to risk the crossing and moored to a
couple of handy bollards on the east bank immediately below the
bridge. While Val prepared supper I walked into the tiny village
and found a pleasant place of neat houses, some adorned with shells
and pebbles of contrasting hues. Stepping into Dennison's the good
lady provided one of the best pints of the journey. Returning to the
river I found a smart blue yacht moored a little astern of us. Apart
from five Emerald Star Line cruisers, this was the first craft we had
encountered since leaving Shannon Harbour more than one hundred
miles away. Feeling as though I was part of some Stanley and
Livingstone re-enactment I introduced myself and was told that the
yacht had been bought in England and was on her way to Dublin.
The young man on board explained that since his wife knew nothing
of sailing he thought that the passage up the Barrow and down the
Grand Canal would be a gentle introduction for her. It would have
been lacking in grace to have informed him what lay in store further
upstream.

The next morning we woke to brilliant sunshine but it was not that
which had tipped us from our slumbers but the clanking churns of

the Avonmore Creamery, which lay hidden behind a belt of trees on the opposite bank. We soon moved off to Lower Ballyellen and then the locks came at fairly regular intervals on the passage to Graiguenamanagh. The river was now entering a more steeply-banked valley and at Borris lock we found that the island which divides the artificial cut from the river was so narrow that wooden platforms had been built out over the waterway so that the boatman was obliged to hang perilously over the swiftly-flowing water in order to get enough purchase on the beam to open the gate. At Clashganny lock men were removing a mound of sand which had been dredged from below the lock and placed on the bank. As we bounced our way out of the lock we decided that they might have dug a little deeper. Above us there was a great sore on the side of the gorge where a wide strip of trees had been removed from summit to riverside. This was to improve the view from a picnic site at the top. It was a nasty bit of official vandalism.

One double lock lay between *Fenniscourt Star* and our overnight mooring at Graiguenamanagh, but at first sight we had doubts that we should be able to progress any further, for one of the middle gates had lost its balance beam. We entered the first chamber, closed the gates and opened the racks to equalise the level of the two chambers. A great deal of perspiration and hauling on ropes lassoed round the gate got it open with much juddering but we then found that our high wheelhouse would not pass beneath the bridge which crosses the lock just below the middle gate. The only way through was to open the lower gate racks to reduce the level, hoping that there would still be enough water over the middle cill to let us pass. The manœuvre was successful and we were soon moving downriver past the long, gentle bend of the Devil's Eyebrow and on towards the town bridge.

Our approach to the town quay at Graiguenamanagh on the west bank was a spectacular and colourful affair. It wasn't that the towns-people had hung out the flags to welcome us but that more than one hundred canoeists were littered across the broad strait through the town. Some of them spent most of their time turning turtle in the water while others were shooting the white water of the weir. It was a training exercise of the Irish Canoeing Union. In conversation with one of the instructors I mentioned that it looked a little dangerous, but he assured me that it was not and that they had only had one broken collarbone during the three-day event. Enough said.

It was Saturday afternoon and, having safely moored, it was not long before we had the usual complement of children lining the riverside. The gang was led by a young man by the name of Kelly who, although only seven years old, spent most of his time extolling the merits of his father's bar and grocery. After a number of conducted tours from the heads to the galley—the business-minded could have made a small fortune out of conducted tours—we cast off and retreated below the bridge to a quieter mooring.

Crossing the bridge from the tiny settlement of Tinnahinch on the east bank to Graiguenamanagh on the west, we also passed from County Carlow, the smallest county in Ireland, to County Kilkenny. Graiguenamanagh (Graig na Manach) is the village of the monks but of their great ecclesiastical settlement, the Abbey of Duiske, little remains. According to Bill Duggan's guide which devotes more space to this place than most books, "over the years of neglect, decay and suppression many of the walls, the great tower and buildings, had fallen and the abbey was gradually absorbed into the houses of the town. Now the hardware shop, the pub, the corn store, the Garda station, actually the heart of the town, beats within the fabric of the Abbey Walls."

At the beginning of the nineteenth century some work was carried out in order to make use of what remained of the main structure as a parish church but the modification had furthered the devastation. As we made our way up the steep hill which forms the main street however, the air rang to the sound of chisel on stone and coming out before the abbey, we found the building surrounded by scaffolding and alive with stonemasons and carpenters. Many of the inhabitants of Graiguenamanagh have bits of the abbey in their gardens, if not under the very foundations of their homes, but those parts of the church which still remain are now being carefully and professionally restored. Unfortunately the work meant that we were unable to enter the building or the churchyard.

Turning down a narrow side road we found a neat terrace of half-timbered cottages which looked exactly like Sussex almshouses.

How they came to be built here we could not discover. Returning to the town we crossed the tiny River Duiske, its white water cascading from boulder to boulder as it dropped steeply to the great Barrow below. The river runs parallel to the main street with the shops and houses opening directly on to it. In order to provide back doors each residence has a small bridge giving access.

Returning to *Fenniscourt* with what supplies we could muster in another of those Irish towns where early closing day seems to be any one but the day officially decided upon, we saw that another craft had locked up through Upper Tinnahinch lock and now lay a few hundred yards astern of us making the seventh craft we had seen since leaving Shannon Harbour. Things were clearly getting busy.

Having failed to obtain tide tables for the tidal Barrow at the local fishing-tackle shop, and knowing that the newcomer had probably come up from the estuary, I approached in the by now traditional Livingstonian manner and hailed the occupants of *Calloo*. Her skipper was Cecil Miller and he not only had a set of tide tables but a pot of tea on the hob and a wealth of navigational details to impart. Val and I sat in *Calloo*'s tiny but cosy cabin with Cecil and his friend Michael as dusk settled on the river and they told us tales of the Barrow before Brendan had taken charge of the works which made our hair stand on end. Cecil has sailed, propelled and bow-hauled *Calloo* up the Barrow, down the Grand and into the Shannon for more years than it would be prudent to mention and is something of a Barrow pioneer.

Hailing from Wexford Cecil makes his way to the Shannon in short weekend stages. He then commutes from his home to a variety of lakeside moorings in order to take part in as many rallies and regattas as possible. A flip through the IWAI newsletter when we returned to *Fenniscourt* revealed that we had been in august company, for Cecil at the helm of *Calloo* doesn't just attend the rallies, he wins them. At the seventh Shannon Rally he had to make do with being runner-up in the mooring test and navigation competition, first prize in the latter having gone to Frank Blake on *Francielle*. But a few years ago Cecil swept the board taking the Premier Award, cabin cruiser, mooring, man overboard, cruiser rescue and boat via canal prizes. It's a wonder they didn't ban the man from entering the Shannon after that.

On Sunday morning Cecil arrived just after breakfast to introduce us to Jimmy Gill, Bill Duggan's sparring partner who still plies the Barrow on a CIE maintenance barge and who, it turned out, had been responsible for recently marking the navigation channel throuhg the Barrow bridges. Jimmy leads a curiously nomadic life for although he has a home in the town, much of his time is spent on board 54M which has been converted to provide the skipper with overnight accommodation by the simple expedient of placing a caravan in the hold. Apart from his recently acquired artistic expertise with a paint brush it was difficult to find out what else Jimmy did as he cruised 54M up and down the river. He did however have a fine voice and a memory for many of the old canal and river ballads, an art which he put into practice in *Fenniscourt*'s saloon that morning. One can only wonder what the good inhabitants of the town thought of Jimmy's rendition of "The Boatman from Kildare" as they passed by on their way from Mass. On our return to Athy for the boat rally Jimmy was to be found holding the floor in many a hostelry, although on that occasion we noticed that his repertoire diminished as the night wore on.

FOURTEEN

Loud the Barrow Waters Roar

THOSE WHO HAD PROMISED us greater and greater splendours as we passed down the River Barrow might well be accused of understatement. Turning our back on Graiguenamanagh we passed through Upper Tinnahinch lock and ran downriver in the quickening stream below the peak of Brandon Hill, its contours rising precipitously from the thickly-wooded west bank. High above us the forest gave way to shrub, gorse and heather. On the eastern bank another jungle of trees and dense thickets rose steeply but to a lesser height. The defile of the river grew narrower until it resembled a vast gorge. At the weir of Carriglead the water foamed and roared in increasing abandon, as though it sensed the freedom of tidal waters. This is the place of the great water, "Uisce More, where loud the Barrow waters roar". The lock is the only remaining one of three which were in use before the river was made navigable above Graiguenamanagh and one wonders how the primitive five-ton barges made way against the current, hauled from the line by men rather than horses. At strategic points on bends along the course of the river you may still see, half hidden in the thickets, the remains of the gear for a cable drum. Even in the days of the Bolinder-powered motor boats it was sometimes necessary to attach a line to these, which were then turned by men with windlasses and so the boat was slowly and agonisingly brought round the bend against the torrent.

Below the lock the entire river seemed embroiled in a last frenzied push for open water as it hurtled over two small weirs which pass across two-thirds of the river, although they do not lead to any canal and lock. Currigaleen Rock narrows the channel again and then the great tree of Bahana Wood makes a nonsense of the boat stream as you sweep out into no man's water to avoid its quivering branches. A final glimpse of the weir, and we were swept into the calm waters of the final cut and the approach to St. Mullins' sea lock.

The village of St. Mullins is one of the smallest and most charming on the Barrow. It lies half a mile below the sea lock, something of a misnomer since the sea is yet thirty miles away, the houses clinging to the steep tumbling banks of the little Aughavaud River which enters the Barrow at right angles beneath a low stone bridge, little more than a culvert, which carries the line to its termination at the Steamer Hole. Opposite the confluence lies The Scar, an evil ridge of knife-edged rocks which bars progress up or down river, except in the period two hours before and after high water. It was as a result of this obstacle that the Steamer Hole was constructed to provide a deep-water mooring for boats waiting for the tide. Today the pool is a mass of lilies and small saplings and in their midst lies the hulk of an old Barrow barge. It was once intended to build a new sea lock below The Scar to make it passable at all times.

No bridge crosses the Barrow here which is unusual since most riverside settlements, often set up where a ford could be built, generally progressed to become bridging points. Due to the rise and fall of the tide, not forgetting the winter floods, any foot crossing at St. Mullins must have been impassable for much of the year. Strolling up the valley through the handful of houses we came out upon The Green which straddles a small hill above the village. A few houses clustered round in a broken circle with the village bar. It was here, in the early evening twilight, that we marvelled at the eloquent beauty of the place. Gazing across the river valley to the escarpment beyond, our eyes were led north along the tree line to the towering naked summit of Brandon Hill. A road edged its way along a ledge, almost on the summit of the scarp. Farmhouses crouched at impossible angles and the sound of cow bells ringing across on the heavy evening air completed the image of an Alpine summer pasture many thousands of feet above sea level. Yet in reality Brandon Hill rises to little more than 1,700 feet and we ourselves were standing only a hundred feet or so above sea level. Behind us the rooks cawed their night song from the trees around the church which lies on the site of a monastery founded by St. Moling who gave his name to the settlement. *The Book of Moling* or *Mulling* is now in Trinity College, Dublin.

Back on the riverbank we waited for the tide and watched the fishermen. Suddenly there was confusion in the water, a rod bent and tautened at the play of a considerable fish. The lucky lad stumbled about the shallows in his brogues and trousers and a friend plunged in with the gaff. A salmon lay on the bank. They came towards us with their catch and as they passed the fisherman nodded and exclaimed: "To think that I was only out looking for shad." I know little about fishing but if our man was looking for shad it was a queer heavy rod he was using for the job.

The Barrow, like the Nore and the Suir, was once a prosperous salmon fishery. Today you are unlikely to see pairs of cots, the nets strung between each boat, on the Barrow. Some say it is pollution that has caused the fish to seek out fresher waters, and they are probably correct. But St. Moling's sleeping habits may have something to do with it as well. St. Evin controlled the habits of the fish on the Nore, St. Moling those on the Barrow. The fish met and mingled and the contrary orders of their guardians were causing such confusion that the saintly gentlemen agreed to meet where the two streams met and sort out their difference. St. Moling arrived early and fell asleep. When St. Evin arrived he ignored the recumbent figure, made his peace with the salmon, and from that day to this the Nore has seen the best of the salmon.

By now the water level had risen sufficiently to let us pass safely over The Scar. While in St. Mullins I had telephoned Dickie Fletcher in New Ross at the suggestion of Cecil Miller. The tideway in that town is used by ships of more than 5,000 tons and since there are few convenient moorings for small craft, Cecil had recommended that I contact his friend, who runs two trip boats, and ask his advice. Dickie had been about to depart with a party for St.

Mullins when I called and we agreed to meet by the Steamer Hole and pass down river in convoy.

On the half mile voyage from the lock to the village we were accompanied by a young man by the name of Tommy whose appearance proved to be more than fortuitous. Left hand down a bit, roared Tommy in good Navy Lark style. We had got this far without the rapped commands of a twelve-year-old and Captain Gardner was having none of it. By now Tommy was working himself into a great lather about nets, floats, cots and salmon and so, although the chart indicated a perfectly straight course past The Scar about one-third out from the bank, I obliged and took *Fenniscourt Star* into a zig-zag route that would have done justice to a destroyer with a submarine on her tail. As I throttled back Tommy directed my gaze to the source of his worries. Following the line of his pointed finger I could just make out the most ingeniously laid salmon net, the blue-black camouflaged floats bobbing gently in our white wake. Poachers, announced Tommy. So much for St. Moling.

We had been but a few minutes by the Steamer Hole when the sound of a powerful diesel could be heard coming upstream and soon the snub nosed bows of the *St. Ciaran* rounded a bend. A former Shannon trip boat, similar in design to many which ply the Thames, she is the larger of Dickie Fletcher's two craft which now make tourist trips on the Barrow, Nore and Suir. Evening cruises, during which a gourmet meal is served, have become a feature of this enterprise which recently received a tourism award. Plans for the remainder of our voyage were drawn up. After following *St. Ciaran* to New Ross we were to take on water at her berth and then continue downstream to moor by an old lightship which lay well in the stream but from which access to the bank was possible by way of floating pontoons.

After *St. Ciaran*'s passengers had explored St. Mullins, we set off. The hills fell back on either bank and now the valley widened with the river occupying the entire floor. Tree-girt slopes still fell to the water's edge with the ridge some three hundred feet above. The deep lush trench twisted and turned and now that the line had ended the splendour of the landscape was only visible to those who came by water. The grey-black stone of a castle turret hung suspended over the cleft. A stark and lonely eyrie, Coolhill. It is the castle around which the famous romantic ballad *Eileen Aroon* is set and from where Eileen Kavanagh fled with the minstrel Carol O'Daly to be married by the Abbot of Duiske at Graiguena-managh.

Soon after passing Coolhill we ran into the long sweeping bend at Ringwood and the valley of the Nore stretched away to the north-west, navigable as far as Inishtioge. It was a tantalising sight but the tide was not set for such a venture. The river became wider as we approached New Ross, the steep banks giving way to flatter land as the warehouses and quays of the port came into sight. After filling our tanks we said farewell to the *St. Ciaran* and her helpful crew and moved to our mooring. From our position low in the water the great soaring hull of the lightship looked a formidable berth. Happily, however, a small low-decked tug lay alongside and were we able to moor with little trouble.

The new town of Ross was established by William the Marshall, Earl of Pembroke, and his wife Isabella, Strongbow's daughter. An important port from the Middle Ages, trade has long been on the decline, although an elaborate dredging programme is now under way in the hope of attracting some of the import traffic, particularly of cars, which now uses Waterford on the Suir. From our berth we could see the harbour master's lodge on the quay and behind it long rows of tall stone and brick warehouses, the lower floors of some converted to shops, which bore testimony to busier days. Our sojourn in the town was to be brief, however, since the land of time enough had become the tide of no return and if we were to keep *Fenniscourt* off the mud and return to Athy in time for the festival it was essential that we should not dally too long.

A group of boys who were playing on the board the *Osprey*, as the lightship was called, provided us with a chilling tale of the Barrow curse. It is said that one of the monks of the town killed a local man and that the citizens marched to the priory to avenge his death. Just as they were about to attack, the monks cast a curse on the people and their river to the effect that it would take three lives each year. Although our mooring appeared secure our path ashore was by way of a rope ladder on to the *Osprey*, across a yawning gap to the

pontoon and across yet another murky chasm to the bank. News of
the curse gave us second thoughts about visiting the town in the
evening.

Before we could further consider the predicament we were hailed
from a dinghy which came alongside. On board were Artie and Una
Corbett, friends of Cecil Miller. The waterway telegraph had been
at work again. They were passing downriver from their barge 60M
which was moored by the road bridge while they converted her to a
floating home. Built in 1929 60M had been reduced to the status of
a dumb barge serving the New Ross dredger. She was bought by
the Harbour Commission who installed her to act as a floating jetty
but three days after she had been put in position she was over-
whelmed and sank. Artie, a retired farmer, had been looking for a
good-sized craft and without more ado purchased the wreck and
spent the next three months bringing her to the surface. Hence her
code name, *Eureka*. As the light was fast fading Artie and Una had
to be off but before departing they recommended that we ignored
the curse and spent the evening in the good company of Matty and
Jimmy, proprietors of Ryan's Bar where the cleanest pint in New
Ross was to be obtained.

Readers may have noticed that I am quite incapable of resisting
such temptations so we made our way acrobatically on to the shore
and entered a grand waterside hostelry. Ryan's Bar serves as more
than just the quayside pub. It's the bus station, parcel office and
calor gas agency. All transactions are carried out over a pint and the
place gives the impression of a station waiting-room with certain
added comforts. It was not long before we were in the company of
Jack Kennedy, a keen local boatman. When we heard that Jack, like
the Corbetts, had bought his boat while she was still underwater –
like buying the end of a piece of rope as one of his friends put it – we
began to wonder if most of the boats on the Barrow were bought in
this condition.

Our passage south from New Ross to Cheekpoint, engagingly known
as the Point of the Fairies from the Irish Pointe-na-sige, and up the
Suir to Waterford and Carrick on Suir, more rightly belongs to a
book on coastal cruising although the passage is possible, with care,

for inland craft. From its confluence with the Barrow at Cheekpoint the Suir runs between low hills and open meadowland. The factories, wharves and cranes of Waterford, bustling with container vessels from every corner of the globe, added excitement to the voyage and provided the only truly industrial landscape of our entire trip. The town presents its best face to the river with elegant Georgian buildings overlooking the wharves which make a pleasant promenade by the riverside. Leaving this ancient Viking city — Waterford is a Danish name deriving from Vadrefiord — we passed back into lush rolling countryside. A stiff headwind put white tops to the waves and we were surprised by the length and depth of the rollers so far from the sea. Our bumpy rolling passage gave way to calmer waters as the town of Carrick on Suir came into sight. It was here that we saw our first salmon cots, crewed by teams of four men and working in pairs. The boats seemed impossibly heavy and low in the water, being constructed from one and a half inch thick larch planks. Today many are powered by outboards but during the fishing they still rely on muscle power.

Once past the fishermen, we entered the town by way of an artificial cut which opens on to extensive wharves. The Suir at this point was one of the filthiest stretches of water we had seen and the stench made us wonder just how successful the fishermen were. The riverbanks and much of the bed seemed to be used as the town rubbish dump. Not for nothing had John Weaving pointed out, when he heard of our intention to pass this way, that Suir is pronounced like sewer. The town of Carrick, the rock of the Suir, was in little better condition than the river. There is an interesting jumble of houses of all periods which from the river appear to be piled on top of each other in the manner of Rye in Sussex. From the main street steep cobbled alleys give access to the waterside. A little paint, a few litter bins and a street cleaner could turn the town into a pleasant mooring for visiting craft, since there is a deep basin by one of the old wharves where craft may remain afloat at all states of the tide.

Carrick's saving grace lies at the end of the main street. It is an Elizabethan manor house built by Black Tom, the tenth Earl of Ormond. Sadly the manor was closed and the caretaker nowhere to be found. Some claim that Anne Boleyn, mother of Elizabeth I and granddaughter of the seventh Earl of Ormond was born in the castle, the scanty remains of which stand behind the house.

Leaving the depressing town we retraced our course downstream to Waterford but, in spite of a plentiful supply of moorings, it was essential that we reach New Ross by nightfall in order to make use of the morning's tide. The great rollers increased as we ran towards the confluence with the Barrow, and with the wind rising from the west I did not look forward to the moment when I would have to bring *Fenniscourt Star* beam on to this sea in order to head her back up towards New Ross. We were half a mile downstream of Cheekpoint before I thought the land had provided enough shelter for the turn and then for ten minutes or so we ploughed, screw screaming, towards the safe maw of the Barrow. Suddenly, through the rail bridge, we were cruising on glass and heading towards Pink Rock, Dollar Point and that berth beside the lightship.

Having moored at New Ross I decided to get the feel of solid earth to calm my rolling nerves. No sooner had I set foot on shore than two gentlemen approached. They looked as though they meant business, though of what nature this should be it was hard to discern. They were dressed partly in nautical uniforms but my mind was on other things at the time.

"Would you be the skipper of the boat that's just berthed?" asked one.

"I would," said I.

One man muttered to the other about it being a smart place to moor.

"And where would you be from?" asked the senior of the two.

"Scotland," I replied.

That did it. As two faces lit up I realised that this was New Ross's friendly customs patrol and that I was no doubt now suspected of smuggling from the Clyde or some such offence. It looked like a night in irons.

First there was our burgee, the Emerald Star Line pennant of green and silver with a green star in its centre.

"Haven't seen a flag like that round here before," said the officer, thumbing through his guide to enemy shipping.

"It's from Carrick," I explained.

"Carrick on Suir?"

"No. Carrick on Shannon."

"But that's hundreds of miles away."

Samuel Beckett couldn't have bettered the dialogue.

Was that expression on the faces of my inquisitors one of awe or straightforward disbelief?

"Anyone else on board?"

"My wife. But she's washing her hair and I wouldn't recommend interrupting her at the moment."

That seemed to clinch it.

"I was just nipping over to Ryan's Bar for a pint," said I, in an attempt to ease the conversation round to something approaching reality.

With that I was waved away with a courteous explanation that such checks were essential. I left them standing on the lightship contemplating whether or not to board *Fenniscourt Star*. As I crossed the pontoon to the shore I could hear one say to the other:

"Not bloody likely."

When half an hour later I returned on board Val told me that she had neither seen nor heard anything of the incident and that we had certainly not been boarded by two customs officials. In fact she looked considerably amused at the incident and asked what I had been drinking in Ryan's, for whatever it was it had done wonders for my imagination.

The passage from New Ross to Athy was as scenically splendid as it had been the week before. Waterways may change their mood at any whim of the weather or tide and it has always come as a pleasant surprise to us to discover how the landscape of a stream seems dramatically different depending on the direction in which we are travelling. The two-day upstream journey which followed was spent partly in the company of Cecil Miller on *Calloo* and Derek Dann and his wife Ida. Derek, managing director of Emerald Star Line, was taking one of his craft to Athy to pay a courtesy visit to the rally.

Travelling in convoy can be a useful way of making light work of lock gates and racks. Cruising along in the company of the managing director of the line who own the craft which you are steering is an altogether different experience. Not that Derek was wearing his management hat during the trip. Indeed he's an enthusiastic boatman himself, having built his own craft, *Karalynda*, in his back garden. His own obvious skill at the helm didn't ease our qualms. Matters were further complicated by my decision to hop out at all the locks and lend a hand with the gates. Val was left to negotiate some of the trickiest locks astern of Derek. Never before did *Fenniscourt Star* pass in and out of locks with such grace, not so much as tipping a fender on the walls. Never before had she made such wide sweeps round hazards or passed so slowly along the narrow canals.

At Levitstown lock we stopped for tea and Val went to work with the rubbing compound and the mop to remove any blemishes we had picked up during our long voyage. Meanwhile I set about stringing endless coils of bunting round the decks. This had been begged from a friendly garage proprietor in Graiguenamanagh. *Fenniscourt*'s entry into the harbour at Athy was to be conducted in style.

The Athy Water Rally began on a Friday evening and was officially opened the following morning When I questioned this somewhat eccentric order of events George Speirs, who had moved his family down to their barge for the duration, explained that the first night's junketings were by way of a warm-up session. George had long dreamed of such an event and was pleased to see it under way, but while it is true that he hoped the event would popularise the Barrow Line and the river, it might also be said that he thought 95B had lain lonely at her moorings for long enough.

Lonely she no longer was. Everything that floated from barge to bathtub was welcomed to Athy and the harbour was lined with a colourful flotilla. Pride of place must go to *Anna*, a barge-builder's dream in beautifully-fashioned timber and a long way from her natural habitat, the canals of Holland. There were other more workmanlike Irish barges present like 39M, 76M, *Sequoia* and *Snark*. While some owners have named their converted canal boats others have preferred to retain the original working numbers. The suffix M was added by the Grand Canal Company when motors were fitted. The B suffix on George Speirs' own boat signified a bye-trader or hack boat which would be owned privately, in this case by the Barrow Motor Transport Company. One of the strangest sights was a catamaran which had actually made the journey from the Shannon by canal powered by an enormous diesel motor strapped across the twin hulls. Cecil Miller was much in evidence with *Calloo* draped in a weight of colours fit to strangle the unwary. The message from the mast seemed to indicate that he had a case of plague on board, had a diver down, was carrying explosives and required immediate assistance.

On the first evening a reception was held in the Rugby Club where we met many of those who had helped us along our way. They had come from Dublin and Wexford, Portumna and Athlone, Killaloe and Carrick. Those whom we didn't know seemed to be related to someone we did and I was soon completely confused by a welter of thirty-second cousins and the like. Half the company had omitted to bring boats with them, so much of the time was spent organising berths here, Lilos there and hammocks wherever they would hang. Brendan arrived to dinner and stayed for breakfast in the company of his sons Daragh and Diarmuid, who spent much of their time conducting bargaining sessions with local publicans over the price of a pint of coke.

On Saturday morning a large black sedan, complete with motor-cycle outriders, arrived at the site of the rally. James Tully, TD, Minister for Local Government, had arrived to open the proceedings from the deck of a barge which had been draped in bunting for the occasion. The brevity of his speech was a wonder to hear. He noted that he stood on water and that the great sluice gate in the skies seemed likely to top up the canal supply at any moment. He would be brief. Apart from the weather, he had observed over many years of outdoor speaking two other pitfalls for the unwary. One was being boring. The other was being boring for long enough to see the gathering disperse to the nearest inn. With that it began to rain. Mr. Tully declared the rally open. We got down to the serious business of the day.

Nooners were consumed at Purcells, we spent the Happy Hour at Doyle's and the evening grog ration was issued at Bapties, a truly remarkable establishment where the landlord was said to know everyone in Ireland. A shortage of glasses was noted throughout the town and the Gardai seemed to have taken the weekend off.

For Val and I the highspot of the event was when 39M, crewed by David Coote and Peter Todd, took off for a trip down the Barrow. The prospect of handling a traditional canal barge, sixty feet long and thirteen feet beam, was something of an ambition of mine and David and Peter welcomed us on board. All went well until I decided that a little reverse thrust would be useful as we came to negotiate a bend by a lifting bridge. 39M's ancient Bolinder did not run to reverse without a great deal of blood, sweat and tears in the engine room. "Brakes" were applied by the simple expedient of nosing her into the bank. What happened if we met another craft coming towards us in a narrow channel? David and Peter simply smiled.

As we lay in the harbour at Athy it was the end of a voyage. Since leaving Carrick we had travelled more than four hundred miles and passed through fifty-seven locks, twenty-six of them twice. In comparison to cruising the canals of Britain, where locks average one per mile, we had been lucky. We were not counting. There comes a time when lock blends into lock as do the blisters on the hands which work them. Why do it? For the scenic splendours? For the peace and isolation away from the hubbub of modern city life with its accent on speed? For the marvels of eighteenth- and nineteenth-century engineering? For the eccentricities of the architecture of bridges and waterside cottages which strew the navigations? For the history, the myths and the legends which attach themselves to any ancient highway? Or the prospect of justifying a great many pints of stout at the end of a hard day's cruising? Every voyager will have his own reasons for venturing into the stream. You will find your own reasons, as we did, in the land of time enough.

Appendices

Appendix A: DISTANCE TABLES

The Shannon Navigation

	Acres Lough—Limit of navigation on Lough Allen Canal											
Battlebridge	3¾	Battlebridge										
Junction with Leitrim River	4½	¾	Junction with Leitrim River									
Junction with River Boyle	8½	4¾	4	Junction with River Boyle								
Carrick on Shannon	9¼	5½	4¾	¾	Carrick on Shannon							
Rooskey	23½	19¾	19	15	14¼	Rooskey						
Tarmonbarry	30¾	27	26¼	22¼	21½	7¼	Tarmonbarry					
Lanesborough	38¼	34½	33¾	29¾	29	14¾	7½	Lanesborough				
Athlone	57¾	54	53¼	49¼	48½	34¼	27	19½	Athlone			
Banagher	80¾	77	76¼	72¼	71½	57¼	50	42½	23	Banagher		
Portumna	93¾	90	89¼	85½	84½	70¼	63	55½	36	13	Portumna	
Killaloe	117¾	114	113¼	109¼	108½	94¼	87	79½	60	37	24	Killaloe
Limerick	131¾	128	127¼	123¼	122½	108¼	101	93½	74	51	38	14

The Boyle Navigation—From limit of navigation on River Boyle to:

Rockingham Harbour	2¼ miles	Cootehall	5¾ miles
Knockvicar Lock	3¾ miles	Junction with River Shannon	9½ miles

The Grand Canal: Dublin to Shannon Harbour

Locks and navigable branches

Circular Line. Ringsend Basin to 1st lock Main Line	7 locks
1st lock to junction with Old Barrow Line	18 locks
1st lock to junction with New Barrow Line	19 locks
Both Barrow Lines navigable.	
Junction with New Barrow Line (Lowtown) to Shannon Harbour	17 locks
Edenderry Branch runs for 1 mile to town harbour	

	Ringsend Basin	1st Lock Main Line	Sallins	Robertstown	Edenderry Junction	Daingean	Tullamore	Rahan	Pollagh	Belmont
1st Lock Main Line	3¾									
Sallins	20¾	17								
Robertstown	28	24¼	7¼							
Edenderry Junction	40	36¼	19¼	12						
Daingean	50¾	47	30	22¾	10¾					
Tullamore	59½	55¾	38¾	31½	19½	8¾				
Rahan	65½	61¾	44¾	37½	25½	14¾	6			
Pollagh	69½	65¾	48¾	41½	29½	18¾	10	8½		
Belmont	78	74¼	57¼	50	38	27¼	18½	12½	8½	
Shannon Harbour	82	78¼	61¼	54	42	31¼	22½	16½	12½	4

(From figures supplied by IWAI.)

The Grand Canal: Lowtown to Athy *The Barrow Navigation: Athy to St. Mullins*

With limits of navigation on Rivers Nore and Suir including part of the tidal Barrow

Locks: Barrow Line . . . 9 locks Barrow Navigation . . 23 locks

River Nore: New Ross to Inistioge. It is not possible to reach Inistioge except on a rising tide. The same tide used to lock out of St. Mullins cannot be used.

	Lowtown	Rathangan	Monasterevan	Vicarstown	Athy	Carlow	Leighlinbridge	Muine Bheag	Goresbridge	Graiguenamanagh	St. Mullins Sea Lock	New Ross	Cheekpoint	Waterford
Rathangan	8½													
Monasterevan	15¼	6¾												
Vicarstown	22½	14	7¼											
Athy	29	20½	13¾	6½										
Carlow	37	28½	21¾	14½	8									
Leighlinbridge	44¾	36¼	29½	22¼	15¾	7¾								
Muine Bheag (Bagenalstown)	47½	39	32¼	25	18½	10½	2¾							
Goresbridge	54	45½	38¾	31½	25	17	9¼	6½						
Graiguenamanagh	63	55½	47¾	40½	34	26	18¼	15½	9					
St. Mullins Sea Lock	67½	59	52¼	45	38½	30½	22¾	20	13½	4½				
New Ross	78½	70	63¼	56	49½	41½	33¾	31	24½	15½	11			
Cheekpoint	88½	80	73¼	66	59½	51½	43¾	41	34½	23½	21½	10		
Waterford	93½	85	78¼	71	64½	56½	48¾	46	39½	30½	26	15	5	
Carrick on Suir	113½	105	98¼	91	84½	76½	68¾	66	59½	50½	46	35	25	20

Appendix B

NAVIGATIONAL DATA AND CHARTS

Sea-going craft may enter the inland waterway network of the Republic at:

Ringsend Basin, Dublin, from the Liffey
For two hours either side of low water the depth over the cill is less than
3ft. There is mooring available below the lock. An overhead pipe, which
cannot be seen until in the lock mouth, means that all sailing craft must
step their mast.

Dimensions of craft which may use the Grand Canal.

      Length   61ft
      Beam   13ft
      Draught   4ft (no more than 3ft 6ins is advisable)
      Height over
        waterline 9ft.

St. Mullins Sea Lock from the tidal Barrow
Access to New Ross is possible at all states of the tide. There are mooring
buoys north and south of the rail bridge above the town. Moorings giving
shore access are difficult to find. Tide-tables covering the Barrow, Suir
and Nore are available from the harbour masters at New Ross or Waterford.

Dimensions of craft which may use the Barrow Navigation.

      Length   61ft
      Beam   13ft
      Draught   2ft 6 ins maximum is advisable
      Height over waterline 9ft.

Navigation authority for Barrow Navigation and Grand Canal—Córas
Iompair Eireann. Lock permits may be obtained from the Canal Section,

CIE, Pearse Station, Westland Row, Dublin 2. The lock-keeper at St. Mullins lives at Graiguenamanagh Lock where permits are issued. A lock windlass is essential. 1¼ins gauge.

Ardnacrusha Lock, above Limerick, from the tidal section

The author has no experience of this, the most difficult point of entry. Inland craft venturing into the estuary should seek local pilotage advice. Incoming craft should contact Ardnacrusha Lock before arrival. The only means of access to the shore is via a 60ft vertical ladder.

Dimensions of craft which may use the Shannon Navigation.

Length   96ft
Beam   19ft
Draught   4ft 6ins
Height over waterline 8ft 9ins for craft coming from the estuary. Otherwise
                the headroom is 16ft above Killaloe. 13ft below.

Permits are not required on the Shannon where payment is made on passage through each lock.

Admiralty charts are available for all the estuary passages. In addition there are two ancient charts of Loughs Ree and Derg (5078 and 5080). They are uncorrected since the original survey in the mid-nineteenth century but special copies are available from the IWAI who have added the most recently buoyed channels. Hire craft are equipped with booklets giving all navigational advice. The navigation authority is Oifig Na nOibreacha Poibli (Office of Public Works), 51 St. Stephen's Green, Dublin 2.

Guides

For navigation data and details of shore services:

The Shannon Guide. Details from Irish Shell Ltd., 20 Lower Hatch Street, Dublin 2. (Provided free to hirers.)

Guide to the Grand Canal and the

Guide to the Barrow Line of the canal and Barrow Navigation. Details from Hon. Treasurer, Inland Waterways Association of Ireland, 2 Clonskeagh Road, Dublin 6.

Ordnance Survey maps. Details from Director, Ordnance Survey Office, Phoenix Park, Dublin.

Further assistance

Membership of the IWAI costs £2 and visiting boat owners are encouraged to join. If contacted in advance the IWAI will give every assistance to visiting owners, whether members or not, and the offer of a shore party to help craft through the difficult Dublin section of the canal is of considerable help.

Hire craft

Emerald Star Line, St James's Gate, Dublin 8. The only company on the canal is Celtic Canal Cruisers Ltd, Tullamore, Co. Offaly. Details of all other hire craft from Bord Fáilte Eireann (Irish Tourist Board), Baggot Street Bridge, Dublin 2.

Other navigations which link with the Shannon

The Ballinamore and Ballyconnell Canal and the Royal Canal are derelict but restorable and IWAI work parties have helped to keep some sections navigable. Small boat rallies have been held on both waterways. The Ballinamore and Ballyconnell runs for thirty-six miles through sixteen locks from Leitrim to Lough Erne and if restored would provide a link with a further 300 square miles of inland cruising water known as Ulster's Lakeland.

The Royal Canal was a rival route between Dublin and the Shannon passing through forty-six locks. Closed to navigation but not officially abandoned some maintenance work is still carried out. Since the last working boat passed through in 1951 the waterway has survived many attempts to infill. There are, alas, a number of low bridge crossings. Restoration is possible and one incentive is that it would provide an excellent round trip route from the Shannon in conjunction with the Grand Canal. The Minister for Local Government, Mr. James Tully, has already intervened to prevent the construction of a culvert. Ian Bath is Hon. Sec. of the Royal Canal Committee of the IWAI.

Appendix C

BIBLIOGRAPHY

Books marked with an asterisk will be of special interest to skippers. Although out of print many of the early volumes about Shannon voyages can still be found in mint condition in Dublin bookshops.

BANIM, Mary *Here and There Through Ireland*, The Freeman's Journal, Dublin. 1891*

BYRNE, Francis John *Irish Kings and High-Kings*, B. T. Batsford, Ltd.

CHADWICK, Nora *The Celts*, Penguin Books

CURTIS, Edmund *A History of Ireland*, Methuen

D'ARCY, Gerard *Portrait of the Grand Canal*, Transport Research Associates, 139 Fortfield Road, Dublin 6

DELANY, V. T. H. and D. R. *The Canals of the South of Ireland*, David and Charles*

DELANY, Ruth *The Grand Canal of Ireland*, David and Charles*

DILLON, Myles *Early Irish Literature*, University of Chicago Press

ENGLISH, N. W. *Lough Ree Yacht Club 1770–1970. A Memoir*. Available from Lough Ree Yacht Club, Athlone, Co. Westmeath*

FLANAGAN, Patrick *The Ballinamore and Ballyconnell Canal*, David and Charles*

GOODBODY, L. M. *The Shannon One Design Class. A History*. Available from Lough Ree Yacht Club (address above)*

GUNN, Neil *The Green Isle of the Great Deep*, Faber & Faber, Ltd. Souvenir Press, Ltd.

HAYWARD, Richard *Where the River Shannon Flows*. 1940 George G. and Harrap & Co., Ltd. 1950 Arthur Barker, Ltd.*

HYDE, Douglas *A Literary History of Ireland*, Ernest Benn, Ltd.

JOYCE, P. W. *Irish Local Place Names Explained*, Fred Hanna, Ltd.*

KINSELLA, Thomas (Translator) *The Tain (Tain Bo Cuailnge)*, Dolmen Press, Ltd. Oxford University Press

MALET, Hugh *In the Wake of the Gods*, Chatto and Windus*

MALET, Hugh *Voyage in a Bowler Hat*, Hutchinson*

O'MEARA, John J. (Translator) *The Voyage of St. Brendan*, Dolmen Press, Ltd.

MERRIMAN, Brian *The Midnight Court*, translated by *David Marcus*, Dolmen Press, Ltd.

PHILLIPS, John *Phillips' Inland Navigation*, David and Charles. Reprint*

PRAEGER, Robert Lloyd *The Way that I Went*, Allan Figgis, Dublin

RICE, H. J. *Thanks for the Memory*. First published 1952. Republished by Athlone Branch, IWAI, Sean's Bar, Athlone, Co. Westmeath*

ROLT, L. T. C. *Green and Silver*, George Allen and Unwin, Ltd.*

SIMMS, J. G. *Jacobite Ireland 1685–91*, Routledge and Kegan Paul, Ltd.